STORYTELLING
FOR LEADERSHIP

Creating Authentic Connections

by

Charles Vogl

APOCRYPHILE
PRESS

THE APOCRYPHILE PRESS
Berkeley, CA
www.apocryphile.org

Edited by Rose-Anne Moore
Book Design by Shaji George
Copy Editing by Steven Hiatt
Cover Design by Annu Yadav
Cover Layout and Figures by James Vogl

ALSO BY CHARLES VOGL

The Art of Community:
7 Principles for Belonging

Building Brand Communities:
How Organizations Succeed by Creating Belonging

To Socheata,
who taught me how brave,
generous, and important it is
to share a true and rich story.

ACKNOWLEDGMENT TO THE ELDERS

This work stands on the shoulders of powerful storytellers and sages who shared with me wisdom gathered over generations. A special acknowledgment is warranted to those who opened my eyes wider. They include Steve Bogner, Allie Perry, Julia Reichert, Mathew Syrett, Cynthia Wade, Ed Zogby—and, of course, the important works by Joseph Campbell and Robert McKee.

CONTENTS

*Some names and identifying details have been changed
to protect the privacy of individuals.*

We Belong to One Another (*excerpt*)

Marvin K. White

The only way that I can know you is
if I know how you are really doing.
I need to know your story
because once I know your story
I can know how you tell it
and I'll know if you believe you are a hero in your story
or a tragic figure.

Then when I have heard you tell your story,
and I know how you're really doing,
then it means I am connected to you.
It means I am responsible to you.
It means that when I see you
I'm looking forward to new plot twists and turns.
Our stories are our connective tissue.
We are blood now.
We are kinfolk.
If we are really in this with each other,
we have to know one another,
deeper than in passing
and deeper than weakly.

THE REASON YOU HAVE THIS BOOK

This book continues my work to support leaders who want to bring people together to make a difference and create cultures of belonging within their organizations. We now live in a desperately lonely time[1], and the skills that connect us grow more precious. In my first book, *The Art of Community: 7 Principles for Belonging* (Berrett-Koehler), I discussed that one of the key principles for effective community-building is the stories that are shared.

Working as a filmmaker taught me the importance of telling stories well to connect, inspire, and draw people together. Telling stories isn't a natural talent for everyone! I had to learn how to tell stories so that others could honestly understand my work and decide if and how they wanted to join me. If I couldn't do that well, then I wouldn't be able to inspire others to accomplish anything with me.

While in graduate school, I realized that other aspiring leaders and accomplished people also wanted to do this better. In our leadership roles, we don't tell stories simply to entertain ourselves or others. We tell them because they're important in our work. We're helping create a future that we can't create by ourselves. We must inspire trust, excitement, and connection in others so that we can collaborate through hard times.

This book got its start one October afternoon at the Yale World Fellows office in a nineteenth-century mansion in New Haven, Connecticut. The Yale World Fellows are innovative leaders from around the world who work across sectors challenging the status quo and developing new ways to tackle very big problems. These mid-career professionals study at Yale for a semester and then return to their work in business, government, and the social sectors. That day I sat at a polished wood table and began leading a seminar called "Storytelling for Change."

Seven of us sat under a vaulted ceiling in an oval room. My students spent over an hour and a half that day learning how to craft stories to present themselves and their vision and to inspire international support.

In the coming weeks together, I would know that they could reliably galvanize a room anytime they wanted and would *always* recognize "*Grocery Shopping Stories,*" literally the most boring and common leader-told story structure I know.

Unfortunately, these shopping stories are the stories that I most regularly hear from company executives, nonprofit leaders, and social change activists on stage, in pitch sessions, and through many dinner conversations. I gave these stories this name because they are structured exactly as shopping stories no one wants to hear.

> First I went to business school.
> Then I started a program in New York.
> Then we hired five staff.
> Then we doubled our outreach.
> Then we set up an office in San Francisco.
> Then we expanded to serve children.
> Now we have four offices and forty-five staff.

These stories are structured in the same way I would tell a story about buying groceries.

> First I went to the grocery store.
> Then I went to the third aisle.
> Then I got whole wheat flour.

Then I got two bags of sugar.
Then I went to aisle seven.

The storytellers may use different verbs and nouns, but no matter. It's the same structure and is always just as tedious. It lacks emotional resonance. It bores listeners, and speakers waste opportunities to share something profound, moving, and memorable. Leaders don't even know they're doing it. When listeners look unmoved and indifferent, storytellers blame their listeners for "not getting it." The storytellers then continue to distance themselves from the very people with whom they most want to connect.

Our training also inoculated the Fellows from ever again using "spaghetti throwing" storytelling—tossing everything they know about their organization, work, or experience into a conversation and hoping that something will "stick" emotionally. They now recognize what builds connection and what can go unsaid.

That fall day we shared the kinds of stories that connect, move, and thrill. We laughed together. Some of us were moved to tears.

When we finished the day's work, Tokunboh Ishmael from Nigeria approached me and asked what further reading I could recommend for study outside class. I paused and considered suggesting thick books by screenwriter Robert McKee or literature professor Joseph Campbell. But I remembered my days working at a Hollywood studio, my work developing exhibition projects for the Smithsonian Institution, and then crafting documentary films in New York. I thought about the hours I'd spent learning about story beside film editors, producers, and directors on three continents. I recognized that I'd gained knowledge over many years from many teachers.

I was surprised that I could think of nothing concise enough for Tokunboh, who was already growing an international investment firm, studying in New Haven, and raising a family. I said, "I'm sorry. I can't think of anything that is right for you because I pieced this together from many books and experiences." Uma Ramiah of the World Fellows office looked directly in my eyes and immediately said firmly, "Then you should write one."

I felt shocked. I thought, "I don't have enough to write a book. Plus, that would take a long time."

Then I reconsidered her words. "Uma sees something I don't or am afraid to. She clearly believes that this would make a difference for global humanitarians who come through her office. What if my book could help them change the world? What if I could make a difference for them?"

Her words inspired me to sit down and write. I'm grateful that she saw what I didn't. In choosing to follow up on her suggestion, I learned to grow committed and supportive in a whole new way, learning a lot about humility, discipline, and the support it takes to bring such a book into the world.

Now this guide is in your hands: it is meant to help executive directors who must gather resources, entrepreneurs seeking to fund the next innovation, change agents who must grow more influential, and many more.

I hope that this book will help my friends and future friends make a difference. I hope that they will share who they are and what they do in ways that inspire others to join them. Simply put, I hope that this little book will change the course of history.

My students tell me that they come looking to tell stories better, and that in the process they find that they also better understand who they are. After all, we can't share who we are until we can say it to ourselves. Some of us are surprised at what we find when we start doing so.

May your stories grow so honest and deftly shaped that they inspire laughter and tears and let others know they are not alone. Or as I think of it: please make laughter, tears, and friendship. The world is hungry for it.

Godspeed.

—Charles H. Vogl
charlesvogl.com

MY STORYTELLER ORIGIN STORY

My professional storytelling life started with an unexpected call one cold November night when I was twenty-nine years old. It was about 8 p.m. and I was sitting in my bedroom on Vernon Blvd. in Queens, New York, when I felt a spiritual call to phone Socheata, then my girlfriend. I felt surprised and curious about this. In the traditions of the Trappist monk Thomas Merton, the Franciscan monk Francis of Assisi, and Missionaries of Charity founder Teresa of Calcutta, there have been several times in my life when no matter what I planned to do, no matter who I planned to be with, or no matter what I wanted others to think of me, God called me to do or be something different. I've learned to be humble enough to follow seemingly innocuous, but strange, calls.

That night, Socheata was sitting in a terminal at Newark Airport waiting to board a flight to Cambodia.

On Christmas Day the year before, in the back bedroom of her parents' home in Dallas, she had learned that for twenty-five years—all her life—her family had been hiding secrets from her. She discovered that her sisters were not really her natural sisters, her brother was only her half-brother, and her mother had lost her first husband and thirty family members during the Khmer Rouge genocide of the 1970s. Socheata wondered what else remained hidden. She immediately planned her first trip to Cambodia to find out.

When Socheata picked up my phone call, I felt a second spiritual call to read the St. Francis of Assisi prayer with her. Here is an excerpt:

> Make me an instrument of Your peace;
> Where there is hatred, let me sow love;
> Where there is injury, pardon;
> Where there is discord, harmony;
> Where there is error, truth;
> Where there is doubt, faith;
> Where there is despair, hope;
> Where there is darkness, light;
> And where there is sadness, joy.

When I finished, I felt the final part of the spiritual call that would change my life. "You will make a film about Love, Joy, and Pardon." When I shared that call with Socheata, it was such a startling and powerful idea that we were both moved to quiet tears.

Socheata and I were about to embark on an intensely personal journey of discovery—discovering both a family's hidden past and our own inner resources. I was a waiter working at a restaurant across from Lincoln Center, and she was a TV production assistant who had just finished a contract with NBC News.

I'd never produced a film. I didn't have a clue about hiring talented people, navigating international licensing rights, or setting up a company to handle film finances, contracts, and a production schedule. I didn't even have a video camera. I didn't even know what I didn't know! Even more concerning, I didn't have a trust fund to pay for an international film production. In other words, I had to start learning everything I could about both creating a film and finding ways to fund it. That learning process filled my life.

A year later, Socheata and I had assembled a small crew, completed two international shoots, and even received a small amount of PBS funding. But I had only raised tens of thousands of dollars, not the hundreds of thousands needed to finish the film—and this was well before Internet-enabled "crowd-funding" was available for such a project. Without more resources, all our efforts and investment would be wasted because an unfinished film is worthless.

I wondered whether I could complete what I had started, or if I was destined to remain an idealistic, but ineffective, producer and leader.

Then, one May night in midtown Manhattan, a wise executive trainer gave me an insight that changed my life. In one simple lesson, he showed me that I was exhausting myself with a "superman strategy." From fundraising to managing a crew to negotiating contracts, I was overwhelmed by trying to master so many vectors to success. Instead, the trainer explained, if I simply focused on one thing, I could exponentially grow my impact and my results. *That one thing was the ability to inspire others to offer up their talent and resources.*

I needed to generate inspiration, connection, and commitment in others. But I didn't know how.

That's when I began to cultivate a board of advisers for my life. This board included a veteran New York political organizer, a high-powered executive coach, award-winning filmmakers, and a wise Jesuit priest who all taught me about inviting the commitment, resources, and skills of others in a deeply authentic way. They coached me on how to build a community, how to connect with others longing to be invited, and, most important, how to share my own story powerfully.

But I was afraid that sharing that this film project actually began in prayer would make others think I was foolish, misguided, or just crazy. Sometimes I wondered if I *was* crazy. On the other hand, I also knew that it was my authentic story.

At a fundraising event that summer, I stood in front of our supporters and volunteers in an upstairs chocolate gallery on New York's Upper East Side and shared the truth about the prayer, my fears, and our intention to change the course of history. I was afraid people would laugh when I told them the truth about the scale of our ambition. Instead, they expressed admiration. Authenticity is so rare in this world that when people hear it, they are moved. Not only did they want to know us better, but they wanted to help us in ways that would stun us.

As my efforts and skills grew, the funding, resources, and talent came together. We beat all the odds against first-time documentary filmmakers.

In November of the following year, in an Amsterdam theater at the largest international documentary film festival in the world, our film, *New Year Baby*, won the Amnesty International—Movies That Matter Human Rights Award on its premiere. We cried again, this time with elation and pride and with our crew.

More important, that night began another journey of sharing the film across the world in order to create healing by unlocking a painful conversation. The film screened from Dubai to Tokyo and from Los Angeles to Tel Aviv, collecting seven international awards along the way. It was shown nationally on PBS stations and on a thirty-city PBS outreach tour. High schools and universities from California to Massachusetts to Texas screened the film to start new conversations. The letters, invitations, and warm reception we received showed us that we were transforming conversations of shame and silence into conversations of honor and heroism. We made a difference for more families than we will ever know.

During a sweltering Southeast Asian July two years after the PBS broadcast, the US State Department ran the film as a special event in the largest theater in Phnom Penh, Cambodia. After that screening, I watched the lobby fill with young Cambodians crowding around Socheata for photos, autographs, and hugs. I listened quietly as they told her that they were inspired to discover their own family's truths after they witnessed how she discovered hers. Just a few years earlier, it had been illegal even to teach about the genocide in school, much less uncover buried secrets. Now these young people wanted to display the same bravery that Socheata had exhibited and know their own families' hidden stories.

I was once again reminded of the power of storytelling. Not only do we understand the world through stories, but we understand ourselves through stories. And the stories that we tell about our lives become our lives.

A leadership story is first a story of self, a story of why I've been called.... You have to claim authorship of your story and learn to tell it to others so they can understand the values that move you to act, because it might move them to act as well.

—Marshall Ganz[2]

STORYTELLING PREMISES FOR THIS BOOK

This guide is written for those who, like me, want to inspire others to join a personal or organizational vision or mission. Your goal is challenging enough that you can't do it alone—and, if completed, will make a difference in other people's lives. We will approach storytelling skill with these premises.

- **Intention.** This kind of storytelling intends to help you create meaningful connections in high-stakes relationships.

- **Authenticity (Truth).** We tell the truth as much as we are able. People will only want to follow us if they believe what we say. As soon as they stop believing us, we lose them. We may fall into the trap of integrity-destroying lies if we think that the truth isn't enough. You will never have to worry about the truth being good enough when you know how to craft a story.

- **Seven Elements.** You will learn the seven elements that make any new story work. With them, you can inspire others and avoid rambling. If all the key elements are included, your stories will work in a one-on-one conversation or on a stage before 100,000 people.

- **Expandable Simple Structure.** The same story can be told in less than a minute or over more than an hour. Most of us want to tell the "same" story in both quick and leisurely ways depending on available time and the audience we are addressing. This guide will give you a structure that will allow you to expand and contract important stories to suit the time available and the audience you are addressing, and help you make them work.

BOOK OVERVIEW

Part 1: Understanding Good Storytelling

Context helps us understand why and when we use stories. If we use them inappropriately, they are ineffective and disappointing. You'll learn what makes a good story "good."

Part 2: The Foundation: Seven Magical Elements

- Setting
- Characters
- Inciting Incident
- Challenge
- The "At Stake"
- Lesson
- Bigger Idea

You'll get introduced to the seven "magical" elements that are the basic elements of good stories. If you don't know what elements make a story compelling, your stories are probably boring, and/or they wander around, hoping to stumble on compelling elements. Once you can identify the elements, you'll be able to see what is missing and what can be thrown away, enabling you to craft a really powerful story.

Part 3: Story Crafting

This section explains how to use the elements to craft a simple one-scene story. Complex is not better; lean is generally better. Once you are good at one-scene stories, you can then develop your skills further with multi-scene stories. You'll learn an easy story structure that allows you to combine your story elements quickly and effectively into a short, purposeful story.

Part 4: Wisdom for the Future

This part gives guidance on how to practice storytelling. Almost everyone underestimates the amount of practice needed for storytelling to sound casual, eloquent, and effortless. I've created a worksheet that you can use whenever you construct a simple and emotionally powerful story.

Appendices

Appendix A: The Worksheet
Worksheets to support story crafting.

Appendix B: Advanced Ideas
This appendix shares advanced ideas to add complexity and nuance to your story *when you are ready*. These are *not* essential elements; please don't try working with them until you are skilled at crafting simple stories. Remember: more complex does not necessarily mean more effective.

Appendix C: Example Stories
I've included real life stories from clients and friends so you can see how they tell their stories in ways that engage and move others. Some stories have dramatic elements; others turn on things that could happen to you any day. I hope you see how each of them would be fun to hear at a dinner or from a stage.

STORY FORMAT NOTE

Most leaders tell stories out loud. We tell stories every day at presentations, meetings, and social events. If you are writing stories for print, then please follow standard grammar and punctuation rules. But if you are *telling* a story, consider using a written format that presents words in the way that you'll say them:

It looks kind of funny
on the page.
It takes lots of room.
This format helps us
"Hear"
the stories,
instead of skimming them
with our eyes.
Using this method,
we break the lines into speaking phrases,
not necessarily
into sentences.
An important word like
"Yes!"
Or
"Really!"
can take its own line.
I encourage you to try it
when you craft stories.
It is way more fun
than writing out paragraphs.
And much more helpful
for preparing spoken stories.

PART ONE

UNDERSTANDING GOOD STORYTELLING

CHAPTER 1

THE LEADERSHIP STORY CHALLENGE

Even the smallest person can change the course of the future.
—*Gandalf, The Lord of the Rings:*
The Fellowship of the Ring[3]

Pursuing any goal that requires followers also requires an aspiration to lead. I advise and train leaders in a wide range of fields. Part of my work involves helping them quickly and powerfully connect with the people who are critical to their success and the success of their mission. These can include funders, staff, volunteers, government regulators, users—really anyone. Obviously one of the most powerful tools we have to make connections is *story*.

For years, leadership trainings have repeated the importance of story. But too many left out the key: what makes a story compelling? Many trainers don't even know why a story often works better than "just the facts," or how a story works, or when it works.

In leadership roles, we use stories to generate emotion, connection, and understanding. But: If someone needs and asks for data, give them the data. If someone asks about your annual budget, and you break into a story, that would be weird. No matter how much you like your stories, give people what they need when they need it.

Consider my venture capitalist friend, whom I'll call Arjan. He knows that when meeting a new prospective investor, the meeting will fail if he opens with a story. Investors first want information about the industry Arjan invests in, his chosen strategy, and his track record. Arjan also knows that once he has successfully completed this introduction, *then* there's an opportunity for an emotional connection, and that opportunity is very important. After all, he told me, investors don't really invest in a strategy, they invest in a person.

In a recent meeting, a prospective investor I'll call Nathana grilled him for lots of relevant data. Arjan apparently responded well. Then Nathana asked, "Why should I invest with you?" So then Arjan briefly shared his personal story of growing up in a small Brazilian city, eventually completing degrees at major American universities, and then using his newly earned status and access to lead the founding and growth of a working hospital in India. His team started with bare land and now the project serves thousands in a remote area each year. Discussing this project, that took years, may have seemed inappropriate — Nathana wasn't going to make a philanthropic contribution to the hospital — but Arjan shared it to make the point that he knows how to succeed even when it means committing to a long and challenging road. He also let her know that he cares about way more in life than growing wealth. He's out to make a difference. Arjan said Nathana smiled and he knew the relationship deepened.

This book will help you tell leadership stories when they can help. Like Arjan, only you can learn when and where stories will serve your relationships and when they will distract.

THE MISTAKES

About four years ago, I worked with a forty-something New York-area CEO who has been featured in national media and already won awards for his work and already won notable awards for his international companies. I'll call him Oliver. He had just been invited to speak at a fairly prestigious New York event, and he was really excited by the opportunity. He wanted to share something deep and encouraging. For hours, we discussed how he could tell a personal story about his formation, how he came to be who he was now. But he was a busy executive, and he didn't practice or discipline his word-crafting nearly as much as I had recommended. On presentation day, his stories wandered around, littered with lots of extraneous detail. Sitting in the auditorium, I didn't know where his presentation was going and I cringed at a cheap joke he inserted. The audience gave him some laughter and applause at the end, and the event organizer told him that he was "great."

Afterward, Oliver took me out to celebrate the day with Southeast Asian food in Lower Manhattan. He told me that he felt good about his performance because he felt confident that he was at least as good as the other speakers.

"Oliver," I said, "we just watched hours of speakers. Can you tell me three points any one of them made?"

He paused, looked up and away, trying to recall what those points might have been, before he had to say, "No."

"That's right," I said. "I can't either. You don't want to play at this level. This is not a crowd to use for comparison. To be at the level you want, you've got to invest and stop judging yourself against this crowd. There is so much more you can do, but they aren't going to tell you that, and they may not even know how totally ineffective they are."

When he reflected on how little he had learned from the other speakers, how boring and rambling several presentations had been, and how satisfied the presenters felt about their performances, he began to understand that the light laughter, friendly applause, and following congratulations are not reflections of quality. Even the worst presenters got that. We don't know if the others huddled with an adviser who shared that the day had been an immense missed opportunity, and that next time could be easily ten times more powerful, with enough attention and application of skill.

Skilled storytelling involves *effectively* communicating ideas and generating feelings. That takes craft or skill. Most stories spoken on a microphone are terribly crafted. Here are some common mistakes:

- Unclear or misguided intention: The teller doesn't know the story's intention—*why* this story needs to be told. (In that case, the listeners won't either.)

- Missing Elements: Tellers leave out critical elements because they don't know what makes a story compelling. (In that case, the story's potential power is diminished or even lost.)

- Story Fat: Tellers include "fat"—unnecessary material that slows or stalls the story. (Include too much fat and listeners drift away.)

When any (or all!) of these mistakes are made, the teller will almost certainly read as incompetent, misguided, or boring. Sadly, most people who seek my help think they're way better than they are. Presentation skills are often a blind spot to people. Almost no one will tell us we are bad at it. This means that boring, misguided, and incompetent stories get told and retold and re-retold. And yet good stories are crucial for leaders.

How can you tell how well you're actually doing? You are probably a poor storyteller if some of the following applies to you:

- You don't know what makes a good story good. (You just know it is good when you hear it.)

- Listeners examine their shoes, hands, or the ceiling when you talk.

- You get polite laughs.

- Few people ask you to share your story.

- You think you are about as good as the others in the room.

The good news is, this is a great area for growth potential and a real advantage — because most speakers are really (really) bad. We'll see if you agree with me by the end of Part 2.

There is no hard-and-fast way to know if post-speech congratulations are honest. I look for very few indicators when I present:

- A follow-up invitation to a bigger or more exclusive audience.

- Someone unprompted giving me their contact information to follow up and connect further.

- An assessment that I was the best speaker in the series that year, season, or ever.

- (*The most important*) People I know who can (and do) recognize quality tell me that I delivered quality.

The common mistakes most often derive from what I call "*spaghetti-throwing*" storytelling: throwing out lots of words and ideas and hoping that some of them "stick" cognitively and emotionally. Speakers who use the "spaghetti-throwing" method don't know what to cut out or what to emphasize because they don't recognize what works.

What if you, just in this chapter, discovered that you have been telling really boring stories? Don't worry. You're not alone. And you have your whole life ahead of you to learn how to tell compelling, emotionally resonant, and powerful stories.

LEADERSHIP STORY INTENTION

Consider what you're working toward and what you want others to understand about the work. To succeed, you need to *communicate* your key ideas and *generate shared feelings*. When you're inviting others to join a commitment, feelings of connection, understanding, and inspiration might be important. This is a high bar for words that may last a few minutes. The *story intention* is the sum of these goals.

1. Communicate key ideas. For example:

- I am relevant in your life.
- We share certain values.

2. Generate specific emotions in others so they will join us in working to achieve a dream. Depending on the overall goal, the feelings we want to realize might include:

▪ Inspiration	▪ Urgency
▪ Connection	▪ Love
▪ Understanding	▪ Concern
▪ Commitment	▪ Shock
▪ Awe	▪ Safety
▪ Excitement	▪ Unification

My guess is that the stories you remember from your heroes inspired something in you. You may even think of those stories with awe and humility. Note that inspiration, awe, and humility are all feelings. Those stories did much more than give you data.

In my experience, creating a feeling of connection is the most overlooked intention of leadership stories. Too many people get caught up in sharing data, and they don't know how to create connection with people they want to work with. You are probably still very connected to the stories of your heroes.

When our stories are purposefully selected for sharing the right ideas and include all seven story elements in a working structure, they can deliver a lot of emotion. But remember that when people want data, give them data.

Among the types of stories powerful leaders (almost) always tell is a personal origin story to explain why and how they are relevant to their field. Organizations also tell origin stories to share how they became relevant and important in their work. The stories serve as capsules that keep and share the values that inform an organization's culture. Origin stories work when listeners understand what happened to change people so that they became committed, effective, or wise in ways that they had not been before. In other words, these stories tell the formation of a leader through experiential lessons that changed her into who she is today.

DEFINING GOOD STORIES

If you're like me, you've sat through a lot of presentations, seminars, and lectures … and remember virtually nothing about the data presented. No surprise—what you remember (if you remember anything) are the stories. The more we improve our storytelling, the more memorable we become, and the more others understand what we've got to share.

For the purposes of this book, a story is a series of selected events that, when put together, explores a journey of change. Describing this change helps us understand an idea or a life lesson.

Story = selected events illustrating change to share an idea or lesson

A story is *not* a collection of everything you know or can find out about an event. Nor is a story just a list of events that happened in the past (we call this *a list of events!*) In this book, both are called what they in fact are: *rambling*. Rambling is boring for the listener and makes the speaker look unfocused and incompetent.

A good story has two qualities: it's compelling, and it has emotional resonance. And it's hard to have one without the other.

1. Compelling

It is compelling if our listeners want to know more. They want to know what happens next, so they will stay and listen. They will get upset if we stop. And they'll share our story with others.

2. Emotional Resonance

A good story generates emotions for the listener—joy or sadness, empathy or rage, or any other emotion … anything so long as it's not boredom. Listeners of a good story get goose bumps; they laugh or cry; they give the storyteller a big hug. The most important feelings we can create with our stories are *inspiration* and *connection*.

You could spend a lifetime mastering ways to generate emotions with stories. But a few simple story elements can quickly help you improve your storytelling dramatically. We will introduce them in Part 2.

CHAPTER 2

EFFECTIVE STORYTELLING

Stories help all of us do at least three important things:

1. Understand and remember.
2. Generate and share feelings .
3. Persuade and influence decision-making by communicating "emotional truth."

UNDERSTANDING AND REMEMBERING

We *understand the world* through stories. Data is important, but it is through the *story* the data lives in that we understand the world. There is a great deal of academic literature about how stories influence our maturation and identity. When we acquire data (raw information), we make a story about it. The stories create meaning that raw data never has on its own. Cognitive psychologist Jerome Bruner writes about how we create meaning through stories. Often stories that are too simple obscure nuance and insight.[4]

This is true whether we are telling "small" stories that help us understand things like these —

- How did my family come to move to California?
- Who is my best friend?
- Where did I leave my keys?

— or whether we are exploring relatively "big" stories that help us understand things like these:

- What is my life's purpose?
- What inspires me most?
- How can I get through the tough times?

Memories formed with strong emotion are retained far better than other memories. This is true both for what is *prioritized to keep in memory* and for the *durability of keeping something in memory*.[5] In other words, we, and our message, become more memorable if we generate emotions (good or bad) in others. Telling an emotionally resonant story can make others remember us—in contrast to the majority of people we all forget.

GENERATING FEELINGS

We have already discussed the importance of generating feelings for leadership. Without training, many people think a story is simply a description of things that happened. Here's an example:

Red Riding Hood took a basket of goodies to her grandmother,
who lived in the forest.
A wolf scared her,
but a hunter saved her.
She and her granny enjoyed the goodies.

Do you want to learn more? Me neither. A straight description of events may technically constitute a story (in a different book), but I promise you that it is never a very good story for our purposes. It is *certainly* not effective for what leaders need to do with stories. Let's make sure our stories generate something that looks like inspiration, connection, understanding, and trust.

DECISION-MAKING

We like to think that we rationally evaluate the available choices when we're confronting a tough decision. But research indicates that our brains make decisions based on emotion.[6] Our emotions choose, and then our prefrontal cortex backfills with intellectual reasoning to justify that decision. We are blind to this process. So the third lesson of storytelling effectiveness is that *feelings meaningfully influence choices.*

Stories give us emotional access or "emotional truth" that data and reasoning cannot. For example, research shows that we do not respond to even major atrocities until we have heard the stories of how individuals have been affected by those atrocities.[7] The stories generate the emotion that then drives our moral outrage and our action. If we're going to spread influence and drive change, then creating emotional resonance through stories will remain crucial because it influences decision-making.

That does not mean that solid data and intellectual arguments are unimportant. We need to understand that *data and intellect alone will not suffice; sharing emotional truth is a key supportive tool.*

CONNECTING IN COMMUNITY

As you have experienced yourself, stories help us make and feel connection with others. This makes creating community possible.

With attention and commitment, communities grow and can drive astounding change. Change within a country, an organization, or a family all starts with our skill in creating individual connections. So crafting stories that support connections is a critical part of what we must do when we aspire to change the world.

CHAPTER 3

YOUR STORY

Before we go on to the steps and elements that make a compelling story, understand how important it is for you to tell your story. If you want to lead anyone, then your followers will want to know about you. They probably won't even listen to you unless you share some fundamental information:

- Who you are.

- What you do.

- How your work matters.

These are really umbrella ideas for more ideas. For example: Under "*Who you are,*" we could include:

- What are your core values?

- Where do you come from?

- Why do you work in your field?

- How are you credentialed, etc.?

Under "What you do":

- Whom do you serve in the world?

- How do you serve?

- Where do you serve?

- When do you serve, etc.?

Under "How your work matters":

- How you are relevant.

- Whom you impact.

- How could the world be different because of you, etc.

Think of leaders who have inspired you, or to whom you feel connected. (They need not be world famous.) My guess is that you know at least one story that speaks to the umbrella ideas I listed above. You probably know several. This is not an accident. Someone took the time to articulate, document, and share those stories so that you could reflect on them now. The elements that make those remembered stories compelling hold true both for our own personal stories and for stories about organizations.

YOUR ORIGIN STORY

A story about how and why you first came to do something is called an *origin story*. If the story is about a person, then it is a personal origin story. Organizations have their own origin stories as well.

You may have several origin stories. For example, I have different origin stories on why I became a filmmaker, why I served in the US Peace Corps, and why I choose to teach storytelling for leadership.

Each story shares a different part of my life and connects listeners to those parts differently. You can do the same.

You should begin your storytelling education by telling your own stories. First, you won't have to do much research because you know your life well! Second, because you know both what is true *factually* (as you remember it) and true *emotionally* (as you experienced it). If you are sharing stories that have real emotional intensity for you, it will be easy to share those feelings with others. My guess is that you'll be surprised how quickly you will learn to share these feelings both powerfully and consistently.

Finally, you should begin your storytelling education with your own stories because these are the most important stories that you, as a leader, will ever tell. If told honestly, they will tell others who you are and how you matter. If you cannot articulate them to yourself, then you cannot share them with others. They will neither understand you nor feel connected to you.

CONSIDER STARTING WITH YOU RIGHT NOW

As we learn the elements and steps for leadership storytelling, consider crafting your story about why you do what you do. You'll be crafting your own origin story. You can choose any area of your life: professional, philanthropic interests, faith, creative work, or your family commitments. These questions may help you get started:

What inspired you?
What are you committed to change?
Why do you think this path was the right one for you?

There will *always* be an emotionally rich story to tease out. Always. You may simply never have acknowledged that story or identified it before. One easy way to find it is to remember a time when you felt tears come up. They can be tears from sorrow, joy, humiliation, thankfulness, or any other reason. Whatever you remember from that time, play with that experience as you develop your storytelling skills.

Once you focus on this story about that experience, you will probably gain new insight into what you want to create and how you might go about it. You may also emerge with insight into which details of the story should be abandoned and which elements need more development. Consider this step before we go to the next section: Name what you're committed to in life. Keep this in your mind as we walk through the story elements. The experiences that inspired your commitments can be shared in a story about how and why you became committed.

Rules for a Personal Story

Since I'm encouraging you to tell your personal origin story, you must know my four rules for telling such stories:

1. Truth.
Tell the truth as you remember it. If someone corrects your facts, then correct the story. If you don't tell the truth, then you look like someone who wants to pretend you are something you aren't. That image erodes your credibility and steals your power and your opportunity to move your listener. Stories have much less impact if your listeners don't fully believe you.

2. Share with an intention.
Have a point. The point can simply be to create a feeling like delight, or to share who you are so that others can understand you. If you're not sure why you are sharing a story, your listeners will be unsure as well. That may lead them to remember you as boring and annoying.

3. Tell appropriate stories for the audience.
Only you can know what your audiences can hear and understand. It is important to remember that there is no one story told in one way that is right for everyone on the planet. For example, MBA student audiences don't often want to hear stories about global religion. Medical doctors include technical medical details when telling a story to other doctors, but they simplify the story for nondoctors. Unless you both choose and refine your story for your particular audience, you will miss many opportunities for emotional connection.

4. Remember that your experiences and lessons are yours.
I've heard many people tell personal stories that inform how they understand the world. I have been told "how religious people think" or "how Asian people act." They are surprised and sometimes angry when I don't agree with the lesson they have taken from their stories. Remember that not everyone—maybe not even most people—will

understand your stories as you do yourself. When someone finds a different lesson in your story, academics call this a "resistant reading." There is nothing wrong with resistant readings. In fact, when listeners share their resistant readings, it is an opportunity for us to learn something new. I'll discuss resistant reading in more detail later in this guide.

Suggested Preparation for the Next Step

- Name something you're committed to in life.

- Write a brief personal origin story, addressing one of the three questions below. (You can address more than one if you like.) Your story can be short—a single page or less is fine.

This exercise simply helps you see how you're telling your story before learning the ideas here, so don't worry about how good or bad your story sounds now.

1. What inspired you?
2. What are you committed to change?
3. Why do you think this path is the right one for you?

Review your story, then put it aside. You will come back to this origin story after exploring the Seven Magical Elements. You'll see your story with new eyes.

PART TWO

THE FOUNDATION:
SEVEN MAGICAL ELEMENTS

CHAPTER 4

A LEADERSHIP STORY'S THREE STEPS

Story crafting is the *third* step in story development.
(In other words, don't get so far ahead of yourself that you trip and fall.)

I've often been approached by executives who seek help with storytelling. We will sit down in a quiet place, and they'll say something like, "I'm doing a bad job telling my story." Or "We need to tell our company story better." Then they will begin some version of the stories they've been telling to investors, regulators, or prospective customers. Almost every time it is unclear to me *why they want to tell this particular story* to the audience they mentioned.

They will look at me across a table and expect me to begin editing their stories so that they'll "sound better." Even the best literary story editors could not help these executives much in getting the results they want, certainly not the most powerful results possible.

That's because story crafting is the *third step*, not the first. If you don't get the first two steps right, then no matter what you craft, you'll be unlikely to get good results. No matter how charming you and your story sounds, no matter how much your audience laughs at your jokes, if your story does not leave your listeners with something emotionally powerful in your developing relationship, it could be a total waste of time.

THE MINIMUM THREE STEPS

Step 1: Name Your Bold Core Message

What have you got that is important enough to say?

If you want to be really compelling, inspiring, and memorable, the first step is to figure out what it is that you have to say that is important enough for other people to hear while awake. I call this your *bold core message* for the world. This is the overarching message that you want the world to understand about you, your work, or your commitment, when all the cute, charming, and novel stuff is forgotten. Whatever story you share will live under and remain connected to this core message.

The bold core message for the world is usually about something we care so much about that we are willing to commit big parts of our lives to its success. We commit our financial well-being, relationships, opportunity costs, reputation, or simply time away from people we love. When an audience hears this core message, they will choose to join us or not. But even if they choose not to join, they will almost certainly respect us for believing in something enough to take a risk and explore the difference we can make.

To consider this from the other side, if you have nothing important to say, if you seek to create no change in the status quo, if you don't care about the future you're creating, then it is possible you actually *are* boring, not just rhetorically boring. If you are indifferent to your own core message, then chances are I'll be bored when you tell me about it.

Identifying this bold core message is by far the most difficult step when I work with leaders. Usually it takes at least an hour with deep questions that are personal, hard to answer, and look like a distraction. Leaders are often caught up in trying to manipulate an outcome with a particular audience rather than inspiring others to get on board.

Example: Irene the Artist

This year I worked with a world-famous artist I'll call Irene. She's invited around the world to create a very specific kind of art. Though she's still under forty years old, her work is already displayed in museums and highlighted in prestigious art books. Artists try to copy her techniques, and they fail. She is the best at what she does, and it took her years to invent her unique style.

After her rise to international fame, Irene experienced a traumatic violent sexual assault that deeply hurt her, sent her into a painful recovery, and significantly changed her art. For most of a year she stopped making art altogether. Recently a filmmaker approached Irene and encouraged her to tell the story of the attack and her recovery. Together they could share the story online.

Irene wondered whether she should take on this new venture. It would almost certainly bring new attention. It might lead to many new invitations to speak about her attack and recovery at important venues around the world. But she wanted to be sure that her story didn't glorify the attack that led to her new and different celebrated art. She didn't want to accidentally glorify the attacker or her painful experience. The subsequent personal recovery and growth had been hard won.

It was clear to me that Irene telling any story about the attack just to get more attention and invitations would fail for her personally. Few of us are compelled, moved, and inspired by someone telling a traumatic story for attention. Certainly, we aren't compelled for long. The irony is that Irene already gets more attention than she feels comfortable with and invitations to more events than she wants to—or ever could—attend.

What mattered to Irene was building more connected relationships with customers, sponsors, mentors, and friends. Her community wants more than a stunt or a car crash to gawk at. Of course, I couldn't know if it would be wise for Irene to share a story about the attack. No one knows how it will affect her career or if she'll feel comfortable when the story is released. My question was this: *What did Irene have to say that was important enough for others to hear?*

People are busy and have lots of media options. There are many artists out there. Some deserve more attention than they're getting. What does Irene think is important enough for others to know?

After about an hour's conversation, what came up was her wish to share hope with others recovering from similar trauma. Her own healing had taken many difficult months. Friends came forward who cared much more than she had ever known. They helped in ways that she never would have predicted, in ways that were often helpful and sometimes not. Nonetheless, they showed her that she was not alone and that she was important to them. These friends helped with the seemingly infinite small steps that eventually got her back to feeling safe and happy, and creating art again, different art because it now reflects a stronger and more mature Irene. *Irene now wants other women to know that it is possible to come back and grow stronger despite fear and pain. For her it happened in part by allowing others to lift her up.* That is worth saying. That is a bold core message that I'll stay awake for.

Only after we could say this out loud did we have something worth sharing a story about. Sharing a story to inspire women, families, and friends to hold onto hope and healing is an entirely different commitment from just getting more attention. What she should say, how she should say it, and possibly even where she would say it, all changed.

As her listeners experience her bravery, they also feel the authenticity behind Irene's words. This is why we named her core message *before* we discussed what and where she would say anything.

Example: Philip the CEO

This year I also worked with Philip, the CEO of a growing men's grooming product company. Philip spent decades in the consumer product industry. For a time, he worked for one of the biggest brands in the field, where cheap chemicals were often prioritized over quality ingredients for the sake of profits. He saw how destructive the industry could be for the environment, and knew the health cost to many consumers who didn't understand how bad the products were for their skin.

Philip started a grooming products company I'll call Niwe. Niwe developed products based on rain forest plants grown, harvested, and processed by local forest communities. By using non-petroleum-based ingredients and tailoring formulas for their customers, Niwe can make money, save rain forests from clear-cutting, employ local people who know these plants, and avoid the physical harm some customers experience when they use big-brand consumer products.

Philip felt dismayed by how little excitement he was generating when presenting to investment groups. He suspected that he wasn't telling the company's story well. The company website included a video showing farmers growing and researchers testing rain-forest plants. Everything that Philip was willing to share inspired a yawn.

In our deep conversation, he revealed that he's building the company because he feels passionate about creating environmentally sustainable products that are healthy for customers and can profitably compete with the industry leaders.

Consumer research showed him that customers wouldn't necessarily buy grooming products just because they were better for the environment. So he said that he wanted his brand to be a kind of "Trojan horse"—products that customers would buy because they liked them and not because they were ecologically responsible. He therefore wanted to hide his ecological values and the company's commitments. But doing so meant that everything he was willing to say made him look no different from anyone else in the industry selling something "new" and "better."

There may be a hundred problems with Niwe that prospective investors see. They will always need to learn that Niwe can and will be a profitable return on investment. And I was confident that if anyone was *ever* going to grow interested in Philip or his work, they'd want to know what was so important for Philip to say in a distracted world. "Niwe's creams are better and from rain forest plants" was not going to do it.

Philip had already risked his whole career on the venture. In our deep conversation, Philip shared that he's really out to up-end how the whole consumer products industry works. *He envisions a revolution where successful investors and executives prioritize sustainability and customer health. This includes selling products safe for many kinds of skin.* That's worth saying. That's a *bold* core message

The story about his own journey to this vision, and about how he gathered the team that has joined him, is far more compelling than everything else he shared. Philip wants to change an entire industry. Of course, stakeholders need assurance that he has the skills, knowledge, and integrity to do that, but those alone will never be enough. Decisions get informed by emotion. For a small new venture like this, new stakeholders must feel connected to him, his commitment and vision.

When he shares his deep vision, he can also share that he's offering specialized workers meaningful work to shift an industry. One investor I know already appreciates that workers with meaningful jobs work more and have greater job satisfaction correlated with increased productivity. [8]

You may now understand how simply tweaking a narrative about product development wasn't going to inspire anyone, certainly the daring investors he is seeking. And even if he effectively hides his message and attracts investors who are only interested in the bottom line, they will make bad long-term partners for this venture.

My Example

Early in this book I shared two personal origin stories. Both are included because I wanted you to understand some things about both me and this work. The first story shares how this book got started. The second shares how I learned to tell and use stories for leadership. Both speak to a bold core message.

The book's origin story:

Bold Core Message: I wrote this book to change the world by helping change makers do exactly that.

My storytelling origin story:

Bold Core Message: Storytelling is a skill that helps struggling leaders build a team that makes a difference, even across country borders.

I'm hopeful that when you discovered those stories you understood that I'm serious about strengthening leadership.

Step 2: Name the Intention for This Audience

Once you can specify your bold core message, you should focus on your intentions for a particular audience. If you're a leader with relationships with funders, staff, customers, and other stakeholders, you may want to speak to each group slightly differently because you have different relationships with each of them. This does not mean sharing honestly with some and dishonestly with others. It does mean understanding what they most need to know about you.

Whenever leaders ask me to help them with stories, I want to know *who they will speak to and what they want as an outcome.* Simply entertaining can be a perfectly good intention, but leaders typically want far more. Leaders want others to join us to help achieve an aspirational outcome. This may include investors trusting us with money, staff bringing their best talents, and customers trusting us to deliver solutions.

When I was a filmmaker, funders wanted to know that I was experienced and committed enough to deliver everything promised at a professional level. My crew wanted to know that I would be honest with them, treat them with respect, and pay them as promised. My volunteers wanted to know that I was honestly motivated and intended to create profound change with the work. For Philip, his investors must learn that he is committed to building a profitable company. His staff want to learn that he is genuinely seeking a safer and more sustainable way to sell consumer products.

It's possible that you will have the same intention for many audiences. For example, all stakeholders want to know that you are committed, that your intentions are honest, and that you have adequate experience to accomplish what you envision.

Ideal Outcome

In the Intention step, we identify the ideal outcome if the time with listeners goes as perfectly as possible. For Irene, it is to create healing. This includes women healing more quickly and with more strength by embracing hope and welcoming others to support their journey. Further, she wants friends and family to offer women the kind of healing support that makes a profound difference.

Philip intends for investors to join his vision to build his company and improve on so many harmful industry methods. He wants them to commit their money and invite their peers to do the same.

Another way to frame your intention is to ask, "What do you want to leave with the listener when you exit the room?" This includes "What do you want them to understand about you or your work that they do not already know?" When we know what we want to leave with listeners, only then can we choose the stories worth telling.

The danger is that we tell stories because we think they are interesting, unique, or dramatic, but such stories may not leave listeners with something that enriches the relationship. If we don't plan ahead, we almost certainly won't get the results we seek.

Example: Randolph the Trial Lawyer and Law Professor

A senior trial attorney, whom I'll call Randolph, reached out to me to help him use storytelling more powerfully. He also teaches trial practice at a law school. Randolph explained that he teaches students to prepare a sad story for the judge and jury about how their own client was harmed. He encourages them to make the courtroom "as sad as possible" in the hope that they will then award a judgment and large payment to his clients.

I think such a simple rule is ridiculous. This advice comes from skipping the first two steps of leadership storytelling. His rule is good only if the intention is to generate sadness in the room.

Step 1: My guess is that Randolph's core message in many rooms can be articulated as something like "Justice is important and we can do something about it here!"

Step 2: Randolph's goal is to inspire a jury to fulfill a vision where the client is awarded a favorable judgment consistent with justice.

When is the last time you did something bold or important because you heard a sad story? For most people this is about never. Feeling concern, outrage, inspiration, hope, satisfaction, admiration, and connection are much more powerful motivators. While sadness may sometimes work for his intention, it will certainly never work for every case in a long career.

I've seen a similar failure in fundraising efforts. I've lost count of the number of times I've heard someone take up a microphone and share stories about the organization's work in the most sober, despairing, and hopeless tones possible. Whenever speakers begin this way, I can feel myself bracing for the next twenty-five minutes. Like Randolph, they do this because they wrongfully assume that others will act only if they feel terrible and that the situation at hand is desperate. Instead of inspiring me to join and commit, such storytelling encourages me to leave the room. I recall one New York City gala supporting girls' education in Pakistan. I feel strongly about educating women, keeping girls safe, and improving whole communities by empowering women—but I had a hard time sitting through that night's presentation. The speaker spoke for well over twenty minutes, sharing about a girl who was denied education, forced to do domestic work, and physically threatened by adults.

In contrast, I recently read an article by Rev. Janine in San Diego, California who's working with other religious leaders. The U.S. Immigration and Customs Enforcement agency drops off immigrant families with young children at a bus station daily. Each family has just completed the legal maximum 20 days of incarceration and is then obviously allowed to remain in the United States.

Rev. Janine wrote about her work with clergy from many traditions to ensure the newly released families get a safe place to stay, bathing access, food, clothes, phone access, bus tickets, and more. Her story emotionally transported me to the scared children coming out of incarceration and the parents trying to keep them safe. When I learned that religious organizations have come together to provide daily support with repurposed buildings and emergency donations, I felt moved and inspired. I remembered that my wife was a refugee. A Texas church helped her find a safe place in the United States and a new life when she was scared. That day I sent funds to support the ministry and the ministers who now inspire me. Then, I reached out to over ten of my friends and invited them to join me.

Supporters are simply members of your community who join you in some specific way. They want to help you *make a difference.*

To accomplish this, they trust you with their money, time and often social capital. Many of us will do this when we are *inspired by the difference you are committed to make*, not because we are depressed by your tragic stories. By spending precious time making us as dispirited as possible, you miss out on sharing the much more exciting, joyful, and inspiring parts of your work. And those parts we're desperate to learn.

Consider the stories from your heroes that motivate you to stay involved. My guess is none of them get you to feel sad and stay there. My guess is that everyone inspires you to stand up and show up like your heroes.

My leaders' storytelling origin story:

Intention: Inspire leaders to learn a skill that will make you far more effective and make the difference you imagine. Success looks like readers learning from the book and practicing for success.

The book's origin story:

Intention: Inspire leaders to join others learning to connect, inspire, and educate, with powerful and as-yet-untold stories around the world. Success looks like readers learning from the book and practicing for success.

Step 3: Craft Your Story

Only *after* we know what you have to say and what you intend to accomplish during your time with listeners can we effectively choose the stories to tell and what elements to include. The remainder of this book speaks to story crafting.

If at some point you don't know what topics, experiences, or memories are relevant to your listener, then go back and review both your 1) bold core message and your 2) intention. Some clarity will emerge. You'll know what you want listeners to retain when you both leave the room.

CHAPTER 5

SEVEN MAGICAL ELEMENTS

You know your bold core message. You are clear about your intention. Now it is time to start crafting your story. The first step in crafting a compelling story is distinguishing which storytelling elements you need to identify. Think of these elements as musical notes. Once you learn a basic octave, you can make millions of beautiful songs by using those notes in almost infinite ways. The seven storytelling elements:

- **Setting:** A specific time and place.

- **Characters:** The people involved.

- **Inciting Incident:** Something happens that causes a thought and feeling inspiring a choice toward a new goal.

- **Challenge:** Things to overcome to achieve a goal.

- **The "At Stake":** The important outcome.

- **Lesson:** Anything (especially wisdom) you learned in the story.

- **Bigger Idea:** How the story affects people other than the hero.

I call these elements "magical" because your stories will magically grow more compelling once you start using them. In fact, you may cause tears. I didn't invent these elements; they come from thousands of years of storytelling. But most people don't know about them, and even when they do, they don't use them well.

These elements are not a formula, because storytellers can use them in many different ways. While I've listed them above in an order we often see, they can be used in any order. Some great stories use only a few of these elements. But if they are new to you, and you exercise your story muscles by using them all, you will see how much more compelling you become. You can make a beautiful song from just a few notes in an octave, and you can make a song with all the notes in that octave. But if you don't know all the notes in an octave, you can't create just the right song.

In *crafting*, you can start with any element. If you know you want to share a story about living in Zambia, then the Setting is probably the right element to use as a starting point. If you want to tell about how you overcame difficult times, then start with the Challenge. After, and only after, we have identified each and all the elements for a story, will it become clear which element you will want to lead with when you *tell* your stories.

Let's not get ahead of ourselves. We must learn some notes before we write melodies.

SETTING

The story's setting has two parts: Time and Place. These are often the first elements we naturally tell in a story. But they don't have to come first.

While this sounds like a very simple idea, many people forget to include a setting at all. The level of detail you include will change depending on the length of your story and your own style. A funny thing about sharing the setting is that often the more specific we are, the more "true" and compelling the story feels. For emotional resonance, we want to share enough about the time and place that our listeners can enter the story with us. If we do our job well, they will feel as though they are actually present in the story.

Place

If you can, consider noting *very* specifically about where a particular incident took place. For example, I could start my story about joining the US Peace Corps in several different ways. Which of the three examples that follow feels most compelling to you?

No setting:
I got a phone call from the Peace Corps office
telling me
"Congratulations,
You've been placed in Zambia."
I felt both thrilled
and scared.
I also thought,
"Now it's real.
I am really doing this."

A general setting:
I was in California
when I got a phone call from the Peace Corps office,

telling me,
"Congratulations,
You've been placed in Zambia."
I felt both thrilled
and scared.
I also thought,
"Now it's real.
I am really doing this."

A specific setting:
I was still in bed
in my apartment on West La Brea and Wilshire
in Los Angeles,
when I got a phone call
from the Washington, D.C.,
Peace Corps headquarters.
I heard,
"Congratulations,
You've been placed in Zambia."
I felt both thrilled
and scared.
I also thought,
"Now it's real.
I am really doing this."

Obviously, at some point, too much detail distracts. You must find your own level. The lesson is to give your listeners enough detail to allow them to easily imagine where you are so that they can be there with you.

Time

Time is similar to place in that, as a general rule, the more specifically you pinpoint it, the more "true" and compelling the story. One important reason is that this communicates that the event is significant for you. We remember the time of significant events: Where were you *when….* ? Ideally, we can share the exact minute when something happened. When listeners hear this, they understand that this moment was really important to us:

> It was 8:04 a.m.
> on March 13, 1999,
> and I was still in bed
> in my apartment on West La Brea
> in Los Angeles,
> when I got a phone call
> from the Washington, D.C.,
> Peace Corps headquarters.
> When I heard the words,
> "Congratulations,
> You've been placed in Zambia,"
> I felt both thrilled
> and scared.

Of course, most of us don't remember the exact minute of much in our lives. I don't actually remember the exact date and time when I got that phone call. I don't even remember exactly where the apartment was. But providing specifics helps listeners put themselves at the scene. So, to remain honest in the telling I could introduce this incident as specifically as I can now remember it:

> I was twenty-five years old in the spring of 1999,
> and living in West LA.
> I was in my apartment there,
> and still in bed
> at about 8 a.m.,
> when I got a call
> from the Peace Corps'
> Washington, D.C., headquarters.
> I was just waking up
> when I heard the words,
> "Congratulations,

You've been placed in Zambia."
I felt both thrilled
and scared.

The point is to pull our listeners into the story with us. Give enough information so that they can imagine themselves in our story.

What Is Enough Detail?

Obviously, at some level, too much detail distracts. You will have to play with what is right for your audience. How much you share within a nine-minute "pitch" will differ from what you include over a four-hour dinner.

When *crafting* a story, I like to get down as much specific detail as possible so that all facts are available to me, then I choose what to keep and what to lose when I practice *telling* the story. If I haven't thought through the details of any element, then I'll be stuck with only general and nonspecific elements to work with. In practicing our stories, we learn how much to share without losing listeners.

CHARACTERS

This is by far the simplest element to learn. Introduce your characters in such a way that listeners understand they are both specific and real. Introductions like the following would not communicate that you are talking about specific, important people:

Somebody
A woman who was there
A guy
A person I could see

The easiest way to introduce your characters is to *tell us their names*. It may sound surprising that names can help. Even if listeners don't need to know the names of characters, sharing them can make those people more real and your story more compelling. "Somebody said to me" feels less real than "Emily Levada said to me"—even if no one in our audience knows who "Emily Levada" is.

Should I include everyone's name? No, especially if your story includes many characters. As with setting, when practicing, explore how much detail to share. Just remember that names can make a difference. When crafting, write many names down so you can use them if you choose. If you don't know a character's name, share other details that make him or her more vivid. For example, instead of introducing a character as "somebody" or "a person," provide some other information. Was this person:

Your mother?
A co-worker?
Your boss?
A complete stranger to you?

If "Brian" is more colorful than "somebody," "Brian, my first CrossFit coach in New Haven" is even more colorful. If I don't know his name, then "my first CrossFit coach in New Haven" is still far better than "somebody."

Or you can tell your listeners what your characters were wearing, whether they were eating, the color of their eyes. Any of these will bring that person to life for your listeners:

> A sweaty guy
> with socks up
> past his knees
> and bigger biceps
> than I'll have in this lifetime
> said to me…

When I'm helping leaders learn story crafting, I'm often shocked how often they leave out available and rich specifics about their characters. When one lawyer shared a life-changing event in her life, she didn't reveal that the person who entered her office and uttered life-changing words was her boss, a firm partner with whom she had collaborated for months. Obviously the story got way more interesting when the character crystalized as more than "someone at my firm." If you're including too much detail, your practice will help you notice.

INCITING INCIDENT

An "inciting incident" is an event that causes a thought and feeling, inspiring a choice toward a new goal. The event *happens in the physical world that changes a character's life.* Many events may set up the inciting incident, but the inciting incident itself happens *in a single moment.* Or, said differently, the listener understands that in a single moment, something changed the character's life.

Stories are made up of *selected* events. Most events aren't included. A good story includes only those events that are significant. Listeners recognize an inciting incident because something happens in the material world *that causes a thought and feeling, inspiring a choice toward a new goal.* Typically the thought and feeling are new so we understand that the choice could not or would not have been made earlier. Ideally, no matter what happens next in the story, the main character cannot go back to the way the world was before the inciting incident. She must move forward, changed by the feeling(s) and choice.

Details about time, place, and characters will help your listeners feel they are right there beside you at the moment of the inciting incident.

For example, if I'm telling my story about moving to Zambia as a Peace Corps volunteer, should I include getting my passport at the post office? How about the phone call I received inviting me to serve in Zambia? Or the conversation I had with my girlfriend before I left for Africa? None of these are important unless I think they are important.

For some people, the official invitation call would be a big deal. For others, after the application, the medical exams, the interview, and the paperwork, the actual phone call isn't so important. So in *telling* the inciting incident, *we must choose which scenes are important and why.* In *crafting* the inciting incident, you may want to include as many moments and details as you can remember.

I could start the journey and my choice to begin in many ways. The weakest way would have no inciting incident:

> When I was twenty-five
> I went to Zambia
> to serve as a Peace Corps volunteer.

Or, I could describe a clear inciting incident where I firmly chose to commit to serve (beginning the journey). I indicate the significance of this moment by sharing a feeling and a thought about the choice:

> On a February morning
> in 1999
> I got a call at 8 a.m.
> from Peace Corps headquarters
> in Washington, D.C.
> When I heard the words,
> "Congratulations,
> you have been placed in Zambia,"
> I felt thrilled
> and scared.
> I thought,
> "Now it's real.
> I am really moving to a place I've never been,
> to learn a new language
> I've never heard
> and to live with people
> who are not like me."

Now, consider that before I got that phone call I had spent months preparing to serve. Those months, the telephone conversations, the medical check-ups, and the essays I wrote were all important events that led to my departure to Zambia. But by selecting a single moment, my story feels more compelling. The listener now understands that I'm committed to a journey to Africa.

What if I don't have an inciting incident?

You do. You just have to recognize it. In all our lives, there are many experiences that change us, and each of those experiences is made up of *many* moments. Pick one moment to represent all the others. For example, when I joined the Peace Corps, there were many moments involved in choosing to serve. There was the moment when I sold my car, the moment when I started packing my bags, and the moment when I picked up my new passport. Each time, I had thoughts and feelings about my Peace Corps commitment. I don't need to share them all; I only need one example to share that experience of choosing.

Emotional Moments

How do you choose the moment? Think back to the moments that made you cry. These aren't only sad times—they could be moments of connection, or of inspiration and elation. Start there because those memories hold a lot of emotion. They may have significantly affected you, maybe more than you've acknowledged before. It will be easier to help your listeners feel emotion when the emotion was strong for you. This is how emotional resonance begins.

If you don't have moments when you cried, then consider sharing moments where you passed from one way of thinking to another, likely with some emotion.

Simplicity

Remember, you can include any moment where you chose to pursue a new goal. The moment you include can represent many moments that together influenced your ultimate commitment. Some moments that could be used as inciting incidents are easier to explain to listeners than others. Some memories involve fewer characters, less necessary context to explain, or are just more familiar to listeners. If it is hard for you to explain an inciting incident to people unfamiliar with your field, then it may be better to choose one that they can understand easily. Confusing our listeners helps no one.

For example, if listeners must understand industry jargon, three preceding events, and/or three possible outcomes from a moment, then that choice is likely not simple enough for most listeners to follow. It will be easier to pick a moment where you can explain the significance in three sentences or less:

> "When I heard the words
> "Congratulations.
> You are placed in Zambia."
> I felt both thrilled
> and scared.
> I also thought,
> "Now it's real.
> I am really doing this."

Don't worry about Interesting (yet). I mentioned earlier that simple inciting incidents can start great stories. If you have an inciting incident that brims with drama, then use it as long as it is honest. For example, you may have stories that start with a plane crash, a snake attack, or surviving acute malaria. Because these are unusual experiences with obvious high stakes, they are more naturally compelling because of the "at stake" story element. Make sure that the incident is honest and relevant to the lesson and bigger idea elements you want to share. If listeners suspect you are simply trying to find an excuse to mention extraordinary events, then you can come across as a show-off, which is obviously not compelling.

Examples

Kelly is a medical student who is also completing a Master's in Business Administration (MBA.) She's becoming a surgeon. She wants to explain to other medical professionals why she's investing time and money toward an MBA. When we worked together she told me about an experience that made her cry. Her story's inciting incident is the moment she noticed a patient's oxygen level plummeting on the surgical table. She realized that she was afraid to speak up because the head surgeon inspired fear in her and others. She thought, "Bad surgical team management kills patients. I want to learn good management to be a better doctor and an example for other doctors." This moment, at least in part, inspired her management education. She and I know this moment held emotion for her because it caused her to cry. When we list story elements, we can write the inciting incident like this:

> I noticed the patient's oxygen level
> plummet on my surgical monitor.
> I felt afraid to speak up
> and thought "Bad surgical team management kills patients."
> I chose to learn good management skills
> and be an example to other doctors.

Grace wants to explain why she works in Nigeria on children's health. Her inciting incident happened while she sat in her high-rise office and read a report that 500,000 children in Nigeria die each year. In that moment she felt shocked and saddened. She decided that she needed to use her business experience to save Nigerian children. We can write the inciting incident element like this.

> I read a report that 500,000 children die
> each year
> in Nigeria.
> I felt shocked
> and saddened
> and decided to use my business experience
> to save lives.

When looking for an inciting incident, remember that they can almost always be summed up in one or two short sentences.

> Where you stumble and fall, there you will find gold.
> — Joseph Campbell[9]

CHALLENGES

The inciting incident inspires the main character to pursue a new goal. The character will face challenge(s) in achieving that goal. Including at least one, and the way your character responds to that challenge, is a key element in getting your listeners interested and emotionally involved.

For example, in my Peace Corps service story, if I share that, while working to build a clinic in Lupososhi, Zambia (goal), I was struggling with undiagnosed malaria (challenge), my story grows more interesting.

If there's no challenge, your story will almost certainly sound boring. I call such stories *grocery shopping stories*. They are as interesting as hearing about a visit to the grocery store:

At 2:20 p.m. last Thursday
my wife asked me to make a cake for that evening.
We got to the Stop & Shop grocery store on Whitney Avenue
about 2:30 p.m.
I parked in the third spot from the door.
First
I went to aisle three
and got some whole-wheat flour.
It was on the second shelf,
right next to the King Arthur bread flour.
Then I went down the aisle about forty feet
and picked up a five-pound bag of sugar.
At the end of the aisle,
I looked to my left
and I saw that the milk and butter
were at the far end of the store…

No one wants to hear the end of this story. Now if I had big challenges finding the ingredients I needed, so that I had to drive to three or four different stores, that might help a bit. It still wouldn't be a great story because it misses other elements, but at least it would sound *more* interesting. Here's a travel "grocery shopping" story:

> First we went to London
> and we saw Big Ben
> and the Tate Gallery,
> and went shopping on Savile Row.
> It was gorgeous.
> We really loved seeing the history in England.
> Next,
> we went to France.
> I loved the pastries.
> We also ate some of the best bread I've ever had.
> The Louvre was just as good
> as we had imagined.
> It was very crowded…

And this too is an entrepreneurial "grocery shopping" story:

> In 1995 we set up an office in Los Angeles
> with just the three founders.
> After only two years,
> we had 10,000 subscribers.
> Then we closed a $1.5 million funding round
> and expanded our program to San Francisco.
> At that point,
> we decided we also wanted to work with children.
> We created a program to work with children
> between the ages of five and ten,
> and now have a staff of twenty-five…

All "grocery shopping" stories follow the same basic structure. They include events or actions without a challenge to overcome. They contain lots of data, but that never makes them structurally interesting. If they're interesting, you got lucky. I consider them the most boring way possible to tell a story—and I see leaders tell them very — very — often.

Think of your favorite stories—not just the epics, but the anecdotes, too. You'll quickly realize that the key character faced a significant challenge in achieving her goal. That's what got you to root for her success: you got emotionally involved in the story.

What challenge should you include?

Anything that keeps a character from achieving their goal is worth considering. Stories from our own lives often include moments when we had too little time, knowledge, resources, connections, or access to achieve our goal easily. These are challenges. Overcoming our personal fears, concerns, and ignorance are also challenges. Did you overcome fear, ridicule, or desperation? If you did, including this will make your story much more compelling and keep you, and your listeners, from getting lost in a grocery shopping story.

Explicit and Implicit Challenges

In some stories, the challenges will appear obvious to listeners. For example, when I share my Peace Corps story and explain that I was going to make a new life in a country I had never visited, speak a language I'd never heard, and live in a village unlike any I'd ever known, it's clear that these will be challenges. This is one reason why a Peace Corps story sounds fundamentally more interesting than actual grocery shopping stories about food buying.

But if a listener cannot easily recognize the implied challenges in our story, we must articulate those challenges to keep the listener engaged. For example, many people do not know that Peace Corps volunteers all have to undergo at least three medical evaluations, almost always complete a college degree, pass an interview, and gain field experience before getting placed. When listeners understand this, their reaction to the invitation call reflects more understanding of what that call meant and the story becomes more compelling.

Explicit information or ideas are those directly stated. Implicit ideas are understood by your listeners from their own knowledge; they don't have to be stated. Both are effective. But if listeners don't have the necessary knowledge to understand our implicit ideas, then we must make them explicit. And if *you* don't know what the challenge is, then your listeners won't either, and they will have to guess. The challenge your listener invents may be very different from the one you intended. This is a mark of a poorly crafted story.

So it's important for you to know what your listeners know or don't know. Explain too much and they'll feel condescended to. ("Everyone knows that!") Articulate too little, and they'll just get confused. ("Why is he telling me this?") Either way, they'll tune you out. This is why we practice to see how listeners respond before we declare a story good.

AT STAKES

An "at stake" is the outcome you want if the lead character reaches her goal. If no unwanted outcome can happen or we don't care about the possible fulfilled outcome, then there's no reason to care about the ending: there's nothing at stake. Some at stakes carry more emotional weight than others.

If I tell a fifteen-minute story about how I drove around to get the best parking spot at the mall (a very low at stake), then you will likely turn away and start examining the ceiling within ninety seconds. But if I tell you that I did this so that my frail Chinese grandmother could get her first Asian meal since entering a senior living facility, then you may pay (a bit) more attention. The at stake got better.

To clarify, the *challenges* are the things that keep the hero from accomplishing a goal. The *at stake* is the *good consequence of overcoming her challenge and reaching her goal.* Of course, stories can still work if heroes fail. The term for these types of stories is *tragedy.* Please know that you can tell great stories where you never accomplish your goal.

Early in this book I shared my own storyteller origin story. It included some of my journey becoming a documentary film producer. When I was producing the documentary *New Year Baby*, my goal was to fulfill a calling to make a film about love, joy, and pardon. The challenges to accomplishing this were 1) fundraising; 2) assembling and leading a crew for the first time; and 3) learning media law (among many other challenges). The at stakes in that story were:

1. Fulfilling a calling.
2. Unlocking conversations about surviving trauma.
3. Family healing.

We know these are the at stakes because *if I didn't* complete the film, I'd have unwanted outcomes.

1. I wouldn't fulfill the calling.
2. The film wouldn't unlock frozen conversations about surviving trauma in communities around the world.
3. The family healing that came from sharing shameful secrets would never begin.

Grocery Story Example

Even a "grocery shopping" story grows more interesting if there is a worthwhile at stake. For example, let's imagine a fictional story where the inciting incident is my wife asking me to make a chocolate cake in the next three hours. My new goal after the incident is to make a cake for my wife.

The challenges are:

1. I don't have ingredients at home.
2. I don't have money to buy ingredients.
3. My car isn't working.

I'll overcome these challenges by:

1. Going to the store.
2. Asking my neighbor Nicole to drive me.
3. And borrowing $30 from her when we get there.

I'll fulfill or fail to reach the goal after facing challenges.

This is a boring story—which is my point. If the at stake is to "get my wife a cake as the whim strikes her," then we all wonder, "Why is he telling this story?" and "Why would I care?" or "Why does he think I would care?" You might also wonder, "Does he know how boring this story is?"

For the purpose of showing the power of the at stake alone, I'll imagine a few other stronger at stakes that are far more compelling. Notice if the story grows more interesting at all.

Original at stake:

My wife gets the cake she wants in three hours.

Stronger at stakes:

Saving my marriage. Showing my wife that I appreciate her after months of distraction from work and nights fighting over neglecting her. I want to show a new side by fulfilling a seemingly whimsical request.

Demonstrating friendship. The cake is for our neighbor's daughter, who is returning from the hospital that very night. She missed her birthday during six weeks spent in the intensive care unit. The cake completes her surprise birthday party on her first evening home.

Fulfilling a promise. The cake is to be delivered to the school's new student dinner, for which we promised to provide a gluten-free dessert by 7 p.m.

None of these at stakes make this a great story. This is partly because the story misses other elements. But I hope you see how including a bigger at stake alone makes this a better story.

Immediate Goal and Bigger Goal

Notice that when I offered better at stakes, the *Immediate Goal* remained making a cake in three hours, but my real *Bigger Goal* was fulfilling what was at stake.

Charles Makes a Documentary Film Example Story

Immediate Goal:
- Make a film.

Bigger Goal:
- Fulfill a calling.
- Unlock conversations about surviving trauma.
- Family healing.

At Stakes:
- Being obedient to a call.
- Truth sharing and understanding.
- Healing.

Martin Luther King, Jr., Example

In March 1965 Martin Luther King, Jr., led a fifty-four-mile march to the Alabama capitol building in Montgomery as part of the American civil rights movement. This story could be told in infinite ways. I'm going to use the basic elements to clarify how at stakes relate to goals.

Immediate Goal:
- Walk to the capitol building and give a speech.

Challenges:
- Violent law enforcement.
- Murderous KKK members.
- FBI harassment.

At Stake:
- To make a rousing speech.

We could say that his rousing speech at the capitol was at stake. This is true because he would miss the opportunity to speak at the capitol if he and others didn't complete the march. But obviously this would miss the much bigger point of his efforts and his journey.

Bigger Goal:
- King's bigger goal was to show Alabama authorities and the whole country that he and his community would resist oppression, expose injustice, and seek equality, all in a nonviolent way. This was all in an effort to create a just, peaceful, and free society for both the current and future generations.

At Stake:
- We could say that the real at stake was justice, peace, and freedom for people who lack all three.

As a general rule, the higher the at stake, the more interesting the story. This is not always the case. After you learn all seven magical elements, you may understand why a story about you finding a rare bottle cap *could* be more compelling than a story about building a village well for a hundred families. As a general rule, however, for leadership storytelling, a story where the at stake is whether your dinner is served on time will be less compelling than whether you were able to serve a hundred dinners to school volunteers.

Naming the *Real* at Stakes

When I work with international executives, thought leaders, and activists, I want them to speak about the honest and bold goals and at stakes they're working on. I'm often shocked by how "small" they speak. Here's a parable I tell to show what a difference it makes when we identify the *real* goal and the *real* at stakes in our work:

The Parable of the Zambian Workers

In my second year as a Peace Corps volunteer
in northern Zambia
I walked deep into the bush
in Luapula Province.
During that dry season
the sun was out.
Children played,
sang,
and called out to me along the trail.
I got to practice my Bemba language
with whomever would talk to me.

I came upon three men working in the sun.
Each wore clothes that were worn to rags
and open-toed sandals caked with mud.
Each sweated profusely from hard work.
I was surprised by their intensity.
I wondered what inspired them.

So I asked the first man
Who wore a broad-brimmed woven straw hat,
"What are you doing?"
He said,
"I'm moving all of these things here,"
He waved his hand at the ground.
"And I'm putting them over there."
He pointed ten feet away,
Where he had in fact placed many things.
"Ah,"
I said,
"That looks like tough work in the sun."
"Yes."
He said.
"I'm committed to success."

I then approached the second man,
who looked like he was doing the same thing
right beside the first.
He only wore a light cap on his head.
"What are you doing?"
I asked.
"I'm clearing this space of rocks,
tree trunks,
and termite mounds."
"There is a lot of stuff here."
I said.
"Yes, there is,"
He said.
"This is an important project for me."

Next I approached the third man.
His actions looked the same as those of the first two.
He worked just as intensely.
He had no hat or cap,
but had simply tied a cloth around his head
To catch the sweat.
"What are you doing?"
I asked.
He stopped,
Stretched his back
And said to me.
"I'm building the first road
from this place, Lupososhi,
to the province capital Mansa,
eighty-four miles away,
So our area can send our farm products to the market.
So we will have money to educate our children
and the next generation
will be better educated
And have more access
to medicine
and doctors
than any generation before."

I looked again
at all three men
working in the Zambian sun.
Then I asked,
"How can I help?

I also have friends,
And I think they'll want to help
When I tell them what you're doing."

I'm sure you felt the difference when the third man shared with me
his *Bigger Goal* and *Bigger at Stake*. And you therefore understand

why the *me* in this story wanted to pitch in after I spoke to the third man. The first two men are perfect examples of the kind of poor at stakes I often see leaders sharing. They share too small when others might run over to help and invite friends if we knew what they are really up to. We want to know what is *really* at stake in this work.

All three men were equally virtuous, hard-working, and honest. But only one shared the *Bigger Goal* so I could understand what was at stake. This is what made a difference. He went from being another laborer to (perhaps accidentally) being a leader attracting followers (me) to fulfill a vision. He did this with his words and honesty.

I'll break down the three men's stories into their elements. Remember, their actions were all exactly the same. How they talked about what they were doing was different.

First Man:
Goal: Move stuff.
Challenge: Stuff is in the work area.
At Stake: A cleared area.

Second Man:
Goal: Clear the area.
Challenge: Rocks, sticks, and termite mounds are in the work area.
At Stake: A cleared area.

Third Man:
Goal: Build a road, increase economic opportunities, educate children, save lives.
Challenge: An eighty-four-mile road must be built in the bush with lots of stuff in the way.
At Stake: Health, education, and likely many lives for more than one generation.

We will discuss the dangers of "talking small" in more detail later in this book, when we review what's important for success.

Clarifying an at Stake

If you are stuck or totally confused about what the at stake in your story is, you can answer the questions below to see if something surprises you, or if there is a far bigger at stake than you imagined. The questions are offered simply to spark your thoughts if you are stuck. If you, the hero in the story, fail:

- Who will get hurt?

- What can you never get back?

- What will it cost—financially, emotionally, politically, healthwise, etc.?

- What will not work?

- What will you miss out on?

- What will you have to do instead?

In our own stories, simply achieving personal fulfillment or a dream is a good at stake. The story could remain self-centered (and therefore boring to others) if we don't use other story elements, but failure to achieve your dream is a perfectly good at stake if you incorporate a strong lesson and bigger idea elements (which I'll present later).

We're not on our journey to save the world but to save ourselves. But in doing that you save the world. The influence of a vital person vitalizes.

— Joseph Campbell[10]

THE LESSON

By far the most important element is the Lesson. The lead character must *learn* something from the experiences of the story. The lesson learned constitutes a change in the lead character. If the story is about you (in, say, an origin story), *you must learn something*. If the story is about an organization, then (you guessed it) the organization must learn something.

You almost always learn something by facing a challenge on the way to achieving a goal. You can also learn something simply from experiencing the inciting incident.

The lesson is the point of the story. It makes the story feel fulfilling. When we exclude a lesson, listeners think, "I wish he had a point." If you don't know what the lesson in your story is, listeners may not either. They may create one themselves. If they do, you won't know what it is, and you may have wasted the opportunity to leave them with a powerful message. If your listeners don't create a lesson, they'll just tune you out.

When the lesson is missing or it is too obscure to identify, few people will ever tell you that you are boring, but you almost certainly are. Again, think of stories that move you, both epics and anecdotes. Do you notice that in each case, the lead character learns a life-changing lesson that will influence her for the rest of her life?

To teach different kinds of lessons, I've named three lesson levels that create different emotional resonance.

Data Lesson

Data is information. This include stuff you learn how to do or knowledge you gain; they are "nice to knows" but not necessarily meaningful. Data is about how something works, or how to accomplish a task because you have new information. For example, I learned the Peace Corps application process, I found out where the Peace Corps office was located, and I learned to speak a new language. These were all useful, and they were all just data. We hear data lessons all the time from mentors and teachers. This is a perfectly good kind of lesson for stories, and by far the weakest for creating emotional resonance.

"To Be" Lesson

In another kind of story, the lead character learns to be a different way. You can learn to be committed, patient, generous, humble, or something else entirely. In every case you learn "to be" different from what you were before. You can learn a lesson of being while also learning a data lesson. "To Be" lessons indicate a true change in your character, and can resonate with listeners, who will have themselves an experience of learning to be a different way (even if their way is different from yours!).

The test to identify this kind of lesson is that it can be shared as a form of "being" necessary to accomplish your goal. For example you can learn to be committed, faithful, creative, or compassionate. You can also learn to be an adult, a teacher, an example, or a friend. There are unlimited ways you can learn to be. When we share these lessons, we share how we formed. We give people a window into who we are now and a reason to see that we are genuine.

For example, as a Peace Corps volunteer, I learned to be patient, to be committed, and to be flexible. I learned these things as I learned a lot of data lessons as well. A story that includes the *being* lessons will resonate more deeply than one that shares only data lessons.

Learning how to be something can relate to a passage toward maturity. Said differently, this type of story describes our maturation. Joseph Campbell is the most famous mythologist of the twentieth century. One of his insights is that one role of myths is to inform us as we mature into stages of life.[11] When we share how we learned to become ourselves, we invite others to understand our passage. It is a very powerful thing. I've seen these stories bring listeners to tears for the right reasons. Listeners feel close and emotionally touched by the storyteller.

When I coach MBA students preparing for their careers or executive directors preparing their pitches, it is a priority for them to share how they learned to be committed, passionate, honest, brave, and more. Well-constructed stories communicate all this quickly and powerfully.

Mythic Lesson

A mythic lesson is the most emotionally resonant lesson. This is a lesson that is learned not only for you and your situation in the story, but a lesson for nearly everyone, everywhere, all the time—in other words, a universal truth. A mythic lesson can move a story closer to mythology. Joseph Campbell shared that mythological stories often represent a character going beyond normal social order.[12] They learn a lesson in a faraway place that makes them far more powerful and wise. For example, you can learn these lessons:

- Compassion leads to stronger cooperation.

- Allowing others to support me is how I accomplish bigger challenges.

- Revealing weakness can be a sign of strength.

These lessons may be true for you in your story and possibly for people in all times and places. With these lessons, the story resonates deeply because it touches the universal.

Another way to articulate these lessons is that you learned "to be" compassionate, humble, receptive, and vulnerable. So there can be overlap with "learning to be" lessons. Most universal truths can be described as a lesson "to be" as well, though not all forms of being lessons are universal truths.

For example, in my Peace Corps experience, I learned that small, tedious actions done in humility can have profound impact. I also learned that the problems of the world are much worse than I had imagined, and that they appear intractable and overwhelming when I faced them by myself. And I learned that people who seemed absolutely different from me in every way nevertheless shared my fears, aspirations, and goodwill. These are mythic lessons.

You do not need to have a universal truth in your story. Just understand that different story lessons resonate differently.

Teaching with Story Lessons

We may share stories because we want listeners to learn something. This is a common and perfectly valid use of story. Keep in mind that it is important to remember that our stories are about what *we have learned ourselves*. If listeners choose to adopt our lesson, that's great … but it may not happen.

I have a much older relative who I'll call Bob. Bob loves to regale me for hours with stories about his life. He expects that I will learn the lessons he lives by and change my life accordingly. Most of the lessons are about how I should invest and grow a profitable business, just as he did. As far as I can recall, Bob has never asked me whether I want to emulate him. Bob and I don't really share similar values about life priorities. I'm no longer interested in listening to his stories because he sounds like he wants me to live his life, not mine.

But I *could* grow very interested in Bob's stories if he shared them as humble offerings of life-changing lessons he learned the hard way. As with Bob, there is a real danger when we tell other people what they should learn from our stories and how they should change themselves accordingly. They (like us) may want to stop listening for perfectly good reasons.

Explicit and Implicit lessons

When you draft stories it is unnecessary to explicitly say, "The lesson I learned is...." Listeners can get the learned lesson even without your spelling it out. It is important that you include a lesson. If you don't explicitly say it, then it's important that that lesson "reads" without your doing so. You know that the lesson "reads" because if you say the lesson out loud, it surprises no one.

If you don't know what the learned lesson is, your audience will search for one and may choose something you don't like or agree with. And keep in mind that if you can't name the lesson(s), it's likely that your story is missing a point.

Multiple Lessons

Any given story can include multiple lessons. For example, if you share a story about learning to sing, you may have learned any of these lessons.

- Many songs can be sung with four to eight notes. (*Data*)
- Your teacher was helpful. (*Data*)
- How to be disciplined. (*To be*)
- How to be patient with growth. (*To be*)
- To be humble in new ventures helps with long engagements. (*To be* and *Mythic*)
- Results come from discipline. (*Mythic*)
- Starting badly is a perfectly good way to start. (*Mythic*)

- Even with simple building blocks, we can creatively iterate. (*Mythic*)

- Learning from experience can make a huge difference. (*Mythic*)

When you draft your story you can choose which lessons you will name or emphasize as you tell it.

A hero is someone who has given his or her life to
something bigger than oneself.

— Joseph Campbell[13]

THE BIGGER IDEA

If a lesson in the story is learned by the heroine, it will change her future because she has become more wise and knowledgeable. Hopefully, it will also change the future of others, perhaps because our heroine has gained wisdom or because of outcomes within the story. *The "bigger idea" is how the changes in the story (the journey) affect people or things beyond the hero:* In other words, the story is "bigger" than just the hero. If the story is about you, then consider how the story could be "bigger" than you. If the story is about an organization, how does the story affect someone or something other than the organization?

In some stories, the lesson has just recently been learned (maybe the day before). Maybe no one or nothing has been affected by the learned lesson yet. As long as someone or something *will* be affected in the future, then you can include this as the bigger idea element.

Great stories are about change. They are often about how we change (mature) as people. For the story to resonate powerfully, we want to know how your change from your experiences (your maturity development) affected someone other than yourself.

If no one else is affected, then the story is a selfish story. It is probably boring and will feel emotionally empty. In general, the more people the story affects, the more interesting the story. But this is not always the case. Changing just one person's life can make for a fantastically interesting and emotionally resonant story.

Last February I trained the marketing staff at a billion-dollar company. While we were working in their top floor conference room overlooking Boston Harbor, one young woman told me that she wanted to tell the company's story, but was struggling with how to do it. When I asked her what she wanted her customers to take away when they heard and understood the company's story, she said (not exactly; I'm changing several details):

"We want to be the biggest retailer of kitchen goods in the country."

This creates almost no emotional impact for the listener. It is an almost perfect example of a selfish intention. Remember the first steps in developing a story: Name the core bold message and name the intention. Why should her customers hear this? Why should her customers care about this goal? This is what is created when we miss the Bigger Idea element.

Unfortunately, lots of organizations get stuck at this basic level. They can't make a selfish message emotionally resonant because they're building on a selfish premise. You can avoid this by including a Bigger Idea. What if we were to add a bigger idea to our marketer's example? Consider these:

- We want to make the most kitchen goods available to Americans with specific and diverse culinary needs.

- We are out to connect the best culinary equipment makers with the people who want their goods most.

- We want to offer customers the most culinary equipment options, no matter their budget or location in the world.

These may not be great ideas, but they're certainly more compelling than the idea she began with. All we have to do is answer the question, *Who else is affected by this story?* When she crafts a story about building a company connecting equipment makers with cooks, then there is the possibility of something really compelling.

Recognizing the Bigger Idea

Maybe you want to tell your story but you don't think you have a Bigger Idea. In other words, you suspect that the only person your story affects is you. If you're telling a personal origin story, and no one else in the world is affected, then you should consider the possibility that your story is selfish, self-absorbed, and boring. It might not be worth telling.

In my experience, though, when we share a story about learning a life lesson, there is *always* someone or something we affect or hope to affect. My students with MBAs who interview at famous investment banks, consulting firms, and start-ups all want to share a compelling origin story about entering their field. They often struggle to identify a Bigger Idea. Some have shared that the lesson they start with is, "I learned I wanted to be rich by...." I promise you: No one is inspired by this story.

When we dig deeper, they often come to see that they want financial success for bigger ideas indeed. Some examples are:

- Providing financial security for their struggling families.

- Ensuring that their family's next generation has access to educational opportunities no matter the cost.

- Making philanthropic commitments that can benefit their community and country.

- Being an example to others that education and commitment will lead to a better life no matter where you start.

There are also bigger ideas for any industry. For example:

- Assuring investors that they have trusted leadership to rely on as they build wealth for their own families.

- Ensuring that customers have high-integrity leaders to turn to for services, healthcare, or advice.

- Providing well-informed and dependable leadership in an industry so it can provide better outcomes than the disasters experienced by the last generation.

- Being an example for those who come next so they can see that commitment and high integrity create results that matter in the world.

It may be tempting to pick a Bigger Idea that sounds good and simply tack it onto your otherwise selfish origin story. Before you try this, consider two things: 1) if you have to do this, you may be a selfish, self-absorbed jerk; and 2) when you tell the story, your lack of authentic emotional resonance with this element will give you away.

Because I don't like to think that *any* of my readers or students are really inauthentic, self-absorbed jerks, let me ask you to take another step. Think through how the lesson you learned could affect anyone other than you (even if the lesson is, "I learned I want to work in private equity"). Surely there are customers, regulators, investors, employees, family members, or others who were affected. If not ... then there are bigger issues in your life to address than better storytelling.

List the people, things, or communities that will be affected after the lesson is learned by the hero in your story. They can all be candidates for sharing a Bigger Idea in your story. You may worry that your stories will sound like bragging. Stories about your success, about the interesting experiences, or about the famous people you know, may be heard this way. Bigger ideas help stories move beyond arrogance and solipsism. Note that if you intend the story to be a brag with a bigger idea tacked on, then it will likely be heard as just a brag.

One of my clients was concerned about sounding nostalgic if she shared how much she had enjoyed working at a university. Would listeners think that she wished she were still at that university? When we worked together, she was able to transcend nostalgia by making it clear that her stories included important lessons that she had learned while she had a job she loved and how those lessons affected other people throughout her life. She showed she wasn't stuck in the past. The past had formed her to make a difference for others in the present and the future.

PART THREE

STORY CRAFTING

CHAPTER 6

MAKING A STORY

SIMPLE CRAFTING

We've covered a lot. Much of this may be new to you, and you may feel overwhelmed. That's OK! Storytelling is mastered over years. In this part, I'll share a simple structure that you can use with the Seven Magical Elements to build a compelling story. The simple structure is of course not the *only* way to build a compelling story. I offer it here because it works even for beginners. Storytelling is like making music. If you learn to sing John Lennon's "Imagine" on key, you can confidently sing it in a living room, at a holiday party, or even in a stadium. If you do it well, it will work fine. You don't have to learn how to sing every Lennon tune in the very first week.

Fat and Lean

A story is, of course, not just a simple list of all seven essential elements. Yet it is extremely important that you can name your essential elements as you craft a personal story.

That is because we want our stories to create emotional resonance, and they do this best when they are *lean*. Lean means that you leave out extra words, clauses, scenes, and distractions. We call the extra parts *fat*. Fat is anything that doesn't help our story read powerful, fun, and compelling. A story is lean when every single word moves listeners from one essential element to another. If we think of our essential elements plotted on a curve, then we want each thing we say to move our listener closer to the next element. This is why we say we want each word to "move the story forward."

When a story is highly focused and clearly moves from one element to the next, it becomes compelling, because the listener is learning what the goal is and how reaching it forms the lead character. When you hang onto every word someone uses, it is highly focused. To get to this you have to know your elements and where you want them to go.

How much of each element should you use?

You can include only as much detail as time allows. If you have five minutes on stage, you obviously can't provide as much detail as you could during a three-hour dinner. Each detail should enrich the story in some way. If it doesn't, cut it out. You must relate enough of your elements so your listener is drawn into the story. *You can expand and contract a story by sharing more or less of your Setting, Character Introductions, and how many Challenges you overcame.* As long as you include all your essential elements, your story should hold together and remain effective, no matter how short.

Three Acts

A good story has a beginning, a middle, and an end. In other words, when we enter the story (the beginning), the world is a certain way. By the middle of the story, the world has changed. And at the end, we understand that the future will unfold differently because of the change that happened within the story. One way to describe this structure is as three "acts":

Act 1: The world as we find it.
Act 2: The change is happening.
Act 3: The change is complete and the future will be different.

What if the world in our story (even a very short one) doesn't change and the future will not be different? Then it's probably a boring leadership story.

Using Three Acts

We are going to use our seven elements in a three-act structure so that we have a beginning, a middle, and an end. One very basic way to do this is by articulating these five ideas.

Act 1:

1. The inciting incident causes a thought and feeling, inspiring a choice toward a new goal.

Act 2:

2. The main character takes an action toward the new goal.
3. A challenge makes reaching the goal difficult.
4. In overcoming the challenge the hero learns a lesson.

Act 3:

5. The new lesson will help others, so the story includes a bigger idea.

CHAPTER 7

SINGLE-SCENE STORY CRAFTING

You can use the Seven Magical Elements in any way that works for you. When teaching people to use the elements for the first time, I prefer to use this simple structure:

- **Setting:** Tell your listeners when and where the story started.

- **Characters:** Tell us who was involved at the beginning.

- **Inciting Incident:** Tell us the inciting incident. In other words, tell what happened in the physical world and what feeling and thought inspired a choice toward a new goal.

- **At Stake:** What unwanted thing could have happened if the goal was not achieved?

- **Challenge:** What could have stopped you, and what did you do to overcome the challenge (if anything)?

- **Lesson:** What did you learn? Was it Data? A "To Be" lesson? Or Mythic? Or some combination of all three?

- **Bigger Idea:** Tell me who is (was or will be) impacted by the lesson you learned and how.

Consider pausing your reading now and try putting these elements together yourself for your personal origin story.

SINGLE-SCENE STORIES

If you follow the steps above, you will probably write what we call a "single-scene story." That means that all the action happened at one time, and maybe even in one place. That's fine. You can think of your story visually like the arc shown in Figure 1:

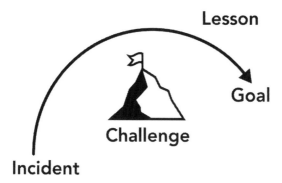

Review your single scene:

- Did you remember to share the inciting incident?

- Did you mention when and where it occurred, and who was involved, so I could understand the inciting incident and the at-stake clearly?

- Did you tell me what goal you wanted to achieve?

I should also understand what challenge was in your way and how you overcame it. When you finished telling your story, I should understand what lesson you learned in overcoming the challenge and reaching your goal. And if your story affected someone besides yourself, then it is even more interesting. If you included all these elements, I'm confident it was, at the least, a somewhat compelling story, even if it was quite short.

EXAMPLE: SIMPLE SINGLE-SCENE CONSTRUCTION

I'll use Kelly's story about learning that she wanted to pursue an MBA. We can see how to break up her story into elements and then combine them using the basic three-act structure.

The example here is a simple "single-scene arc" story. In one scene, Kelly can share how she was inspired to study business management in addition to becoming a surgeon. Kelly can't tell this story in a compelling, lean style until she has figured out what her essential elements are.

Kelly's Essential Elements

1. **Setting:** November 2009. One week from Thanksgiving. Third-floor surgical room at Gryffindor Hospital. Standing eighteen inches from the patient and beside monitors.
2. **Characters:**
   Kelly—medical student
   Chief Surgeon — name withheld, fifty-one years old, male.
   Patient — name withheld, woman, thirty-three years old, needs mass removed.
   Anesthesiologist — Scott, male, thirty-five years old.
3. **Incident:** I noticed the oxygen monitor indicated that the patient was dying. I thought we needed to stop the surgeon from closing the incision. I felt afraid to speak up.
4. **Goal:** Save the patient's life from an apparent complication unrecognized by the head surgeon.
5. **Challenge:** The surgeon doesn't listen to me. I fear punishment and humiliation for questioning the surgical procedures.
6. **Lesson Learned:** Surgeons who inspire fear in their team hurt and kill patients. They cause pain for families. Good management skills will save patients' lives and ease patient

and family pain. I want to learn management skills to be a better surgeon and reform this field and its authoritarian culture.

7. **Bigger Idea:** If I learn to manage my teams well, I'll serve patients better and save families a lot of pain. I can also become an example to other surgeons and help them save lives this way.

Now that she has figured out the elements, she can craft the story. When Kelly shares this story with colleagues and patients she can tell it like this:

Simple Single-Scene Structure

Setting:
In November 2009,
a week before Thanksgiving,
I was on Medical School surgical rotation.
At 3 p.m. I was in a surgical room
on the fourth floor of Gryffindor Hospital in Hartford, CT.
I stood eighteen inches from a patient
watching four monitors during an eight-hour surgery.

Inciting Incident:
As the chief resident (character introduction) sutured up the incision,
I noticed a monitor indicated that the patient's oxygen dropped suddenly
and bubbles came up through the surgical wound.
I was surprised and frightened.
I thought we should stop the closing to investigate a complication
but the chief resident kept closing the incision.

Goal:
I wanted to keep the patient safe.

Challenge:
But I was afraid to speak up
because the surgeon didn't seem to respect me.
He had already yelled at me seven times during that procedure.
The whole staff was afraid to speak.
I knew something had to be done
But I was afraid of humiliation or punishment.

Action to Overcome Challenge:
I remembered I was there for the patient first.
I braced myself
and alerted the surgeon
to both the monitor and the bubbles.
He dismissed them both
as normal.
I then showed Scott, the anesthesiologist.
He saw something was wrong
And called over his staff.
He agreed there was a problem
and insisted on reopening the patient.
When they did,
they discovered a mistaken lung puncture.
Obviously, it needed attention.
The patient could have died if we had missed it.
Even as it was, her recovery took weeks longer. (*at stake*)

Lesson:
That day I learned that surgeons who manage their teams poorly
harm
and can kill patients.
They cause a lot of pain for families.
I decided I need to learn good management...

Bigger Idea:
so all my patients are safer
over the decades of my career.

Further,
I aspire to be a better example to my colleagues, who will also manage teams.
I don't know how many families we can save.
I'm hopeful it will be thousands.
I went to business school because that is where they teach management
and I know the future of medicine
needs the best management skills possible
to save the lives entrusted to us.

Expanding and Contracting Single-Scene Stories

You can *expand and contract single-scene stories by simply sharing more or less detail.* You know the story is stronger when you include all the magical elements. You also know it will stand on its own. You can choose how much detail you include in any one element. As long as your detail strengthens an element, it is likely pertinent to your story. For example, Kelly could choose to contract her story if she only has a few seconds to say something like this.

Simple Single-Scene Structure

Setting:
In 2009
I was on surgical rotation in medical school.
I was assigned to watch monitors during surgery.

Inciting Incident:
As the chief resident sutured up the incision,
I noticed a monitor indicated a sudden oxygen drop
and bubbles came up through the surgical wound.
I was alarmed
and thought we should stop the closing

Goal:
to keep the patient safe.

Challenge:
But I was afraid to speak up
The surgeon had already yelled at me seven times during that procedure.
The whole staff was afraid to speak.
I was afraid of getting humiliated or punished.

Action to Overcome Challenge:
I got the courage
And alerted the surgeon anyway.
He dismissed it as normal.
I then showed the anesthesiologist.
And at his insistence
they reopened the patient.
When they did,
they discovered a mistaken lung puncture.
The patient could have died if we had missed it.

Lesson:
That day I learned that surgeons who poorly manage their teams harm and can kill patients.
A team of trained and talented people are not good
if they are too scared to contribute
or can't contribute.
I wanted to learn good management…

Bigger Idea:
so my patients are safer
Further,
I want to be a better example to my colleagues who will also manage teams.
I went to business school because that is where I found management training.

When I read this aloud, it takes about a minute. Kelly can now tell a one-minute story that shares how she was inspired to get an MBA.

Expanded Single-Scene Story. Kelly can also expand this story if she likes by *adding more detail* to the setting or character introduction. She can also expand the challenge and even the goals to include more than one for each. You may not think the story is better this way, but it is a way to relate more if she has more time and the right audience.

Setting:

In November 2009
I was on surgical rotation
At Gryffindor Hospital in Hartford, CT.
I was only in my third year of medical school
so I was still in the early stages of learning how doctors
and medical staff
work together when someone's life is on the line.
I really wanted to make a good impression, of course,
but I also knew that someday I'd be in charge of a medical team.
When I started,
I remember how seriously I took the responsibility
for keeping someone alive
while they're on the surgical table.
I still do, of course.
It was all just new to me.

It was the week before Thanksgiving
at 3 p.m. one day and
I was in a surgery
on the fourth floor of Gryffindor Hospital.
I remember I stood only eighteen inches from the patient
while she was out.
And I was assigned to watch four monitors
for the eight-hour surgery.
I remember how tired we all got after a full day concentrating.
I remember how relieved I got when we were close to the end.

Inciting Incident:

After all those surgical hours
the chief resident sutured up the incision.
I noticed one of my monitors indicated the patient's oxygen suddenly dropped.
I also saw bubbles come up through the surgical wound.
This is obviously unusual
and I was surprised and frightened.
Of course I thought we should stop the closing to investigate a complication,
but the chief resident simply kept closing the incision.

Goal:

I wanted to keep the patient safe.

Challenge:

But I remember I was afraid to speak up
because I thought the surgeon didn't seem to respect me
or my contribution.
He had already yelled at me seven times during that very procedure.
I knew the whole staff was afraid to speak.
I knew something had to be done
and I was so afraid of humiliation or punishment.

Action to Overcome Challenge:

I remembered I was there for the patient first.
I closed my eyes,
Breathed deeply
and braced myself
to alert the surgeon
to both the oxygen monitor reading
and the bubbles.
Unfortunately,
No surprise.

He dismissed them both as normal.
He didn't even ask me why I thought this was important.

So,
I didn't want to give up.
I thought,
"What else can I do?"
I then showed the reading to Scott, the anesthesiologist,
because I thought he might also see this was a problem.
He did
and called over his three staff.
They talked
and agreed
there was a problem.
So Scott insisted on reopening the patient.
This is what convinced the surgeon to pay attention.
When they did reopen,
they discovered a mistaken lung puncture.
Air was coming out of the lungs
and escaping into and through the surgical wound.
Obviously it needed attention.
The patient could have died if we missed it.
Even as it was, her recovery took weeks longer.

Lesson:
That day I learned that surgeons who manage their teams poorly
harm
and can kill patients.
And there is no reason for it.
I knew this was possible before,
But when I saw it firsthand,
I realized how ridiculous it was.
I knew there is no reason
a trained team
needs to fear
taking care of a patient,

Including pointing out problems
that need handling.
A team of trained and talented people are no good
if they are too scared to contribute
or can't contribute.
Surgeons who create that kind of environment cause a lot of pain
for families,
And I don't even know if they see it
or care.

I decided I need to learn good management…

Bigger Idea:
so my patients are safer
over the decades of my career.
I can't even know what a difference this will make.
Further,
I hope to be a better example to my colleagues who will also manage
teams.
I don't know how many families we can save.
I'm guessing thousands.
I went to business school because that is where they teach
management,
And I know the future of medicine
needs the best management skills possible
to save the lives entrusted to us.

PRACTICE WITH SINGLE SCENES

When you are first using story elements and structure, start by practicing one-scene stories. They can be *very* powerful and easy to tell, and sharing them will teach you what your listeners like.

In fact, now that you know what elements make a one-scene story compelling, you may see that many stories told at length can often be told more powerfully as a one-scene story. In many cases, all the words leaders use to "introduce" a story can (and should) be cut away. Often a single scene of learning or insight is all that is needed—and is much more interesting.

THIS SHOULD BE THE END

If you read no more of this book and get good at telling single-scene stories that are compelling, lesson-filled, and formative for you, then you will be among the top 10 percent of storytelling leaders. Part of me wants to end this book right here because giving you more will not help you if the remainder confuses and overwhelms you.

Simple stories work *beautifully*. If you tell three simple single-scene stories in a row, that will convince most people that you are an unbelievably good storyteller. In fact, if all you ever do is simply line up good single scenes as we have discussed so far, you may need nothing more to share what you will ever need as a leader.

But leaders often want more, and there may be a time when you are ready to become even more sophisticated in your storytelling, so I'm including more. Please do not let the remaining ideas scare, confuse, or frustrate you.

CHAPTER 8

MULTISCENE STORY CRAFTING

At some point, you will want to learn to tell longer stories. A long story can be crafted simply as a *series of compelling single scenes.* This is one reason why learning to tell single-scene stories well is such an important first step.

If each scene includes all the magical elements, then listeners will have a hard time walking away. Together, the string of scenes will explore the lessons you have learned over time. Listeners will understand your formation as these lessons combine and they will feel moved by the story.

OVERARCHING ELEMENTS

Bigger stories are simply structurally bigger versions of a single-scene story. They have their own goal(s), at stake(s), and lesson(s). Each *scene* has a goal, an at stake, and a lesson, and the story of *all the scenes* has a goal, an at stake, and a lesson. We call the elements that remain the same for the whole story "overarching." This is simply because they stay with the listener throughout the whole arc of the story (through all the scenes). I'll provide examples below.

Overarching Inciting Incident

Earlier I discussed the importance of including an inciting incident so listeners know what inspired a journey of change. When we use more than one scene, it is OK to share an inciting incident in the first scene that begins the journey. This is the first act. When we add scenes (in the second act), we do not need to include an inciting incident in each scene. The character can simply take action toward her new goal and learn something in each scene. When the opening inciting incident inspires action toward a goal for the whole story, we call this an overarching inciting incident.

Overarching Inciting Incident: The moment that inspires pursuit of a goal for the whole story. Including an overarching inciting incident means that we do not have to include an inciting incident in each scene in the second act. This is because a choice is made that changes the life of the hero.

Multiple Inciting Incidents

You can include additional inciting incidents that inspire your character to change goals or pursue some new way of overcoming challenges. For example, Kelly wants to learn management skills so she can be a better doctor. She will take many actions to overcome challenges to do this. These include: 1) finding a way to learn management; 2) paying for it; 3) scheduling the time; and 4) handling the skepticism and disdain of more senior doctors. These do not need a new inciting incident because they are all challenges in pursuing the same goal.

She could also share experiencing something (like a conversation) that inspires her to earn an MBA in particular instead of simply taking leadership seminars. This experience (the conversation) is an inciting incident for her new (bigger) goal (get an MBA, not just management seminars.)

Overarching Goal

When we add scenes to a story, listeners stay interested if there is a *big goal we are working toward.* They stay around to discover whether we will achieve it (or not). We call this goal throughout the story an *overarching goal.* This goal can be presented as a question. In Kelly's story it could be, "How did she learn starting an MBA program was right for her?" We call these questions that remain across the whole story *overarching questions.*

Think of stories like *The Lord of the Rings.* This is an epic with many —many — scenes. However, in any given scene we know that Frodo wants to complete something in the current scene (for example, survive an attack by the Black Riders) *and* he has the bigger goal of saving Middle Earth. We can present and think of each goal as a question.

Immediate question: How will Frodo survive this attack?
Overarching question: How will Frodo save Middle Earth?

The scene and story will only remain interesting if the scene helps answer both questions. This sounds more complicated than it is. For example, if Frodo learns how to survive this attack (say, by using his Elvish armor), he will obviously progress toward answering how he can continue (or fail to) save Middle Earth. Staying alive and overcoming obstacles (including attacking orcs) help him to save Middle Earth.

Overarching Goal: The goal that our main character is trying to reach through all the scenes.

Overarching Question: A question that each scene of a story is helping to answer. Wanting to learn the answer to the question keeps listeners interested.

Immediate Goal: The goal for the character in a particular scene.

Shifting Goals

It is totally fine for a character (you) to start with one goal, and then learn a lesson in a scene that changes your goal. In fact, this is often part of the best stories. This shift to a different goal can be a great part of a character's formation. The character changes from wanting one goal to pursuing a different goal. Depending on the goal shift, this can be part of your maturation. Making a goal more specific or broader is a common feature in epic stories, and it's a perfectly good feature for you as well.

Remember that for each goal shift, you will need to share an inciting incident that caused a thought and feeling that inspire the choice toward a new goal. This is where sharing more than one inciting incident in a story is important.

Expanding Goals

A character can have a simple goal, and in facing challenges and learning, *the goal expands to something bigger and more challenging.* For example, in *Star Wars*, Luke's original goal is simply to rescue the princess. On his journey, he changes his goal to ending imperial oppression.

For a startup CEO, the original goal could be to help her own child with a medical problem, but after experiencing and learning more, she chooses to help all children in the world with the same problem.

Refocused Goal

On the other hand, a character may start with a big goal and learn through experience that she really wants something *very specific and focused.* My friend Emily runs a nonprofit that works on human rights for refugees. When she started her career she wanted to help bring human rights to people all over the world. She has since learned that she wants to focus on helping refugees in displacement camps with their legal rights. Emily still cares about human rights generally, but her experiences taught her to choose and focus.

Changed Goal

A character starts with a goal and then *discovers that it isn't the goal she wants after all.* She chooses and pursues a new goal, entirely different or even opposite from her original goal. The film *Little Miss Sunshine* is a great example: the characters initially work together toward the overarching goal of getting Olive to a beauty pageant in California to compete for the Little Miss Sunshine title. Late in the film, the characters discover that not only do they really not want Olive to compete in the competition, they don't want to be associated with the kids and families in the pageant world. They discover — learn — that what they really want is to stick together. They want to create a supportive family, and they do this at the pageant.

A social change leader could start a career with the goal of becoming a high-powered attorney and then discover that what she really wants is to ensure that justice is accessible to as many people as possible, even if that means giving up a managing partner title or a traditional career path.

The changed goal is often the most satisfying goal change in a story. But *this is not a reason for you to invent one.* It is often satisfying because the character must at least implicitly acknowledge that she was mistaken about what she wanted in the world before she matured on her journey.

Don't Worry Too Much about the First Scene's Goal

Because characters can learn and change their goal within a story, it is not important in a multi-scene story that there is a clear vision in the beginning of who you will be at the end. I have students who want to tell how they got into a certain field. They tell me there is no single moment where they chose their field, but a series of small progressions. A story can accommodate the process of choosing over time.

Below is the actual story goals progression of one of my students, Gideon, who works in investment banking. The overarching question for Gideon's story is "How did Gideon choose finance as the right field for him?" I'll summarize a story he can tell colleagues, senior partners at firms, and even customers. When he tells his story, he can share a series of scenes that demonstrates how he learned to choose each goal below.

Summary: Gideon grew up in a poor Chinese village where his family didn't have enough food or heat through the winter. He didn't even have warm enough clothes. He studied and worked hard so he could grow rich enough to escape his village hardships. His goal was not very generous, inspiring, or noble for the world. Of course it wasn't. He was cold and hungry. However, as he learned more, his goal of what he could do with his education, experience, and access expanded. He learned how corruption, greed, and instability in the finance sector were harming the wealth of all the Chinese people and keeping inspired, hard-working entrepreneurs from making as big a difference as they might. This journey expanded his understanding of what he could accomplish and what was really important to him. Gideon now knows that tens of millions of Chinese died from starvation just a generation ago, in large part due to poor economic policy. Now that he's learned about economic policy, entrepreneurialism, and innovation, he is really concerned about how economic policy is affecting China's future. He wants to influence policy for the whole country. His story is about the formation of his goals: from helping his family escape poverty to taking on much bigger challenges.

Gideon's Goal Progression

Kid Goal: Be rich enough that my family is warm and has plenty of food.

College Student Goal: Get the best grades. Stand out. Get the most prestigious attention and job offers.

Young Entrepreneur Goal: Learn how to build a profitable firm. Gain credibility.

Business School Goal: Excel in classes and internships to get a job in a prestigious and high-paying firm.

Working Professional Goal: Make the finance industry safer for customers, fairer to start-ups, and a trusted partner in China's economic expansion for the next generation.

I share Gideon's story goals as an example to show you that a story that doesn't sound very inspiring or emotionally resonant because the early goals are limited (maybe even selfish) can still end powerfully because the goals change in later scenes. The goal can change even in the last scene. When a character's goal changes like this, we call it maturation. In Gideon's story, he matured from caring mostly about himself and his family to caring about an entire generation of Chinese. If it weren't a true story, then this would simply be a manipulative work of fiction, and eventually, Gideon would be uncovered as a fraud and a liar. (But in this case, his story is all true.)

Overarching At Stakes

If you are uninterested in the overarching question in any story, you will obviously become uninterested in the story. This is true in epics as well as personal anecdotes. Remember, if there is nothing at stake that we care about, then we typically do not care.

So to keep stories relevant and listeners interested, we need overarching questions that our audience cares about. You may not be interested in Kelly's overarching question, and you may not care whether or not Frodo saves Middle Earth. This doesn't mean that the stories are bad (or that you are bad), it means you are the wrong audience. You simply care about other things.

Senior partners in medical firms, hospital executives, and Kelly's own staff will be *very* interested in her story. Her answer to the overarching question will share Kelly's formation and her values. Her story tells us that she values serving patients and making medical teams work well more than she cares about looking good or getting punished by dangerous, vindictive, and self-satisfied senior doctors. This is why it is important that she learn to tell this story honestly and well.

As long as a character (you) is taking action toward your goal, facing a challenge, and learning something in each scene, there will be dramatic tension and listeners will remain interested. One way to think of dramatic tension is presenting the questions about if and how characters will resolve their problems. If there is a really big question, there will be more dramatic tension.

When we share our goals, the at stake is important, because without it no one cares if we accomplish our goals. *The at stake validates the efforts to achieve the goal (and the effort to listen to the story).*

Overarching At Stake: The at stake that validates efforts along the whole story.

Immediate At Stake: The at stake in any one scene.

Overarching Challenge

When you tell stories with multiple scenes, the first scene will set your character on her journey toward a goal that has challenges to overcome. Each scene will be about your character working to overcome those challenges. There may be an overarching challenge to overcome that you will not need to re-articulate in each scene. Because the challenge wasn't overcome earlier, listeners will understand that it is still present in the story even though you don't mention it in each scene.

For example, in Kelly's story about learning that doctors may harm patients because they manage their teams poorly, she will go on a journey to find out how she can learn better skills than she found in her own medical training. Later I'll share an expanded multiple-scene example of Kelly's journey. I won't have to tell in each scene that the challenge is finding how to learn better management skills. You will understand that that challenge remains until she resolves this issue or gives up.

Overarching Challenge: The challenge that remains in the story until it is resolved or abandoned. It does not need to be articulated repeatedly as long as listeners know it is still present.

Overarching Lesson

We already know it is far more interesting when characters learn (or "form") in each scene. They do this by facing a challenge of some sort. When we craft stories with multiple scenes, it is important that the journey across all the scenes provides an overarching lesson (or lessons). These lessons collectively make the characters different at the end of the story than they were when they began. This is the change that makes a story worth telling.

I can tell a (fictional) story about me extinguishing a fire in an elementary school. I could tell you how hard it was to get the kids out, find water, and get back to the fire with the water. I could even go on about how I ruined my clothes. The at stake would obviously be the safety of the other kids and maybe the school's existence. Keep in mind: to make a good story it is not important whether I succeeded in saving the kids or the school. We hear lots of stories that involve failure. What makes the story worth hearing is how I, the other kids, or the school were changed after this experience. Centering the story on the at stake(s) of my efforts to fight the fire makes sense, but if I end the story without sharing how someone was changed or "re-formed," then the story will fall flat.

My point here is to help you understand that at stakes are important, but the lesson(s) learned are more important. We call lessons or formation that happens over the whole the story *overarching lessons.*

Overarching Lesson(s): The lesson(s) learned from the whole journey or several parts of it.

Immediate Lesson(s): The lesson(s) learned from a particular scene or action, overcoming a particular challenge.

Remember, no matter what you think, the internal growth (formation) of the hero is the most important part of the story. If you miss this, it will never matter how good your other elements or structures are: your story will never emotionally land.

Overarching Bigger Idea

Just as with a single-scene story, we need a bigger idea element to keep a longer story from sounding selfish and self-absorbed. In multi-scene stories, however, we can save the bigger idea element until the end of the whole story and not necessarily present it in each scene. The bigger idea for the whole story is an overarching bigger idea.

Overarching Bigger Idea(s): The way(s) the entire story in total (not one scene) affects people other than the main character.

When we craft a story that will end with an overarching bigger idea, it is less important, or unimportant, for any given scene to articulate a bigger idea. Your character (you) can learn selfish lessons in many or all the scenes, and then share an overarching bigger idea at the end of the story. You can include this in an epilogue (a type of end summary). The overarching bigger idea can be something only understood after all the scenes have been experienced.

For example, in the story of Gideon, the Chinese finance professional, it is not immediately clear ,during the scenes of his studying and working to make money, how his story (his maturation) will impact people other than himself. However, as he matured into an educated and experienced professional, he recognized the importance of honest and wise finance professionals for the welfare of millions. He then committed his career to keeping China's economy healthy so it can serve at least the next generation without risk of mass starvation. Gideon doesn't need a bigger idea in each scene. He can sum up his bigger idea in the end.

MULTISCENE FORM

When telling a longer story is appropriate, we can simply expand the structure we know for single-scene form. The same arc of a single-scene story can expand to bigger stories while maintaining the three-act structure.

Act 1: Opening: The world as we find it.

Act. 2: Main Body: The series of challenges overcome and lessons learned in your story before achieving or failing at the goal, share the main lesson and bigger idea.

Act 3: Closing: The change is complete and the future will be different.

A single-story arc has these elements in this structure.

Act 1
- Setting.
- Characters.
- Inciting Incident (which inspires action toward a goal).

Act 2
- Action relating to a Challenge.
- Lesson(s) Learned.

Act 3
- Bigger Idea that will affect others.

Multi-scene Formation

If we want to expand the story, we can add scenes to the second act that explain how you took more actions toward the goal and learned something new. When the scenes are lined up, you are sharing a *series of lessons learned*. In doing this, you are *sharing your formation as a leader*. This is often what people most want to understand about leaders. They also want to understand similar things about organizations, projects, groups, and communities.

Why would anyone want to hear about this formation? Because they want to learn how you have had a bigger impact in the world with your completed formation to date. To make your formation and bigger impact clear for the listener, it can be helpful to add a summary of your overarching lesson(s) and future impact. This summary, or epilogue, acts as a third act. This is the part of the story where we understand that the world will be different in the future because of the story events.

Experienced and practiced storytellers may not have to explicitly articulate the overarching lesson(s) learned or the overarching bigger impact. They may all read implicitly. But until you are really practiced, it's wiser to say them explicitly to be sure that your listeners understand them.

A multiple-story arc includes these elements in this structure:

Act 1
Scene 1 (Opening)

- Setting
- Characters
- Inciting Incident (which inspires action toward a goal)
- Action toward goal overcoming a Challenge
- Lesson Learned

Act 2
Scene 2 (Main Body)

- Setting
- Characters (if needed)

- Inciting Incident (if goal shifts)
- Action toward goal overcoming a Challenge
- Lesson Learned

Scene 3 (Main Body)

- Setting
- Characters (*if needed*)
- Inciting Incident (*if goal shifts*)
- Action toward goal overcoming a Challenge
- Lesson Learned

More scenes can be added here…

Act 3
Summary (Epilogue)

- Overarching Lesson Learned
- Overarching Bigger Idea

We can graph it in the form shown in Figure 2.

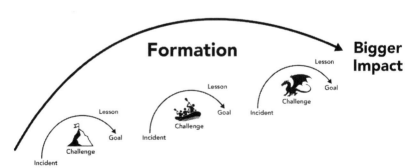

You can add as many scenes as you like as long as your characters are taking actions toward achieving their goal, facing challenges, and learning something. It is not important that characters achieve their goal. It is simply important that they learn. The lesson could even be how hard it is to accomplish the goal.

REQUIRED ELEMENTS FOR EVERY SCENE

You will almost certainly need to include the following elements in every scene to make a compelling story work. Elements can be implied (unsaid) as long as you are sure that listeners understand them.

- **Setting**: We must know where and when you are in every scene.

- **Goal (from the inciting incident):** We must know why you are doing anything in the scene. The reason can be a continuing pursuit of the overarching goal.

- **Challenge**: We need to know what challenge you are facing.

- **Lesson**: We *must* understand that you learned something (even if it is only implied).

REDUNDANT ELEMENTS FOR ACT 2 SCENES

The first scene in a story often introduces elements we don't need to repeat later because listeners know they are constant. You do not have to include these elements in each scene unless it is important for us to understand the challenges faced and lessons learned.

Inciting Incident: Because the first inciting incident sends the character on the journey, it may not be important to introduce a new inciting incident in each scene. It may be enough that, in each scene, the character is taking an action toward the immediate and overarching goals.

Characters: We need to know which characters are important in each scene, but we don't need detailed descriptions in each scene if the characters recur. When you introduce new characters, we will want to get a sufficiently vivid introduction so that we feel that they are real.

At Stake: Because there is an overarching at stake for the whole story, it is less important that every scene explain what is at stake. We will want to know why you are choosing to share this particular scene. Presumably the lesson learned in the scene will make this clear.

Bigger Idea: Simply sharing an overarching bigger idea at the end is plenty. You can share this in the Act 3 epilogue.

GAPS AND GUTTERS

This is a fairly sophisticated principle that I want you to understand, but it's one that should not distract you from simple story crafting.

When choosing scenes and linking them together, you may worry that your listeners will get lost if you simply introduce a new scene in a new time and place. This will not be a problem if you have an overarching goal and at stake. If you learn a lesson in a new scene that helps you toward the overarching goal, then audiences should understand why the scene is included.

You want to be clear—but not too clear: audiences want to figure out for themselves how scenes connect. They want to bridge the gaps, and when they do, the story can feel far more interesting to them. When a listener discovers for herself why you included it, listening is more fun.

The best example of this *gaps* principle is found in comic books. Comics tell stories, of course, and they do this entirely by asking readers to connect a series of still images in their mind. Without readers making the story in their mind, there is no story. Consider this series of images:

- Dog running.

- Dog jumping and looking up.

- Dog head with Frisbee in mouth.

These images tell a story only if *we* fill in action between the images. In comic books, the space between the images is called a *gutter*. The story is really created in the gutters, because this is where readers fill in the action. What comic book artists look for is the sweet spot where the image sequences are not so detailed that they become tedious but not so disconnected that we get lost trying to follow the story.

The same principle holds true when you tell a story with multiple scenes. Not only can you avoid explaining why you included a scene, the story will become tedious if you do link scenes too tightly.

Try simply putting scenes in a row with no linking explanation. Tell strong scenes that stand on their own, with an explicit or implicit lesson, showing how you are pursuing a goal. See if listeners can follow you. If they get confused, you can simply add explanation as needed.

Go to the multi-scene example story about Kelly below. You'll see that I included scenes without linking them to what happened next. I depend on your understanding of the overarching goal and the at stake to let you understand why I'm including them.

Example Multiscene Story

Let's expand Kelly's origin story this way.

Scene 1 [opening]

Setting:
In November 2009,
a week before Thanksgiving,

I was on medical school surgical rotation.
At 3 p.m. I stood in a surgical room
on the fourth floor of Gryffindor Hospital in Hartford, CT.
I worked eighteen inches from a patient
watching four monitors during an eight-hour surgery
To remove a tricky mass.

Inciting Incident:
As the chief resident, Dr. Lyons, (*character*) sutured up the incision,
I noticed that a monitor indicated the patient's oxygen dropped suddenly
and bubbles came up through the surgical wound.
I remember I was both surprised and frightened.
I thought we should stop the closing to investigate a complication,
but the chief resident kept closing the incision.

Goal:
I wanted to keep the patient safe.

Challenge:
But I was afraid to speak up
because the surgeon didn't seem to respect me.
He had already yelled at me seven times during that procedure.
The whole staff was afraid to speak.
I knew something had to be done,
but I was afraid of humiliation or punishment.

Action to Overcome Challenge:
I remembered I was there for the patient first.
I took a deep breath
and braced myself.
Then I alerted the surgeon
to both the monitor and the bubbles.
He dismissed them both
as normal.

I wondered how I could get my monitor readings taken seriously.
I then showed Scott, the anesthesiologist.
He saw something was wrong
And called over his three staff.
He agreed there was a problem
and insisted reopening the patient.
When they did,
they discovered a mistaken lung puncture.
Obviously it needed attention.
The patient could have died if we missed it.
Even as it was, her recovery took weeks longer. (*at stake*)

Lesson:
In that surgery I learned that surgeons who manage their teams poorly
harm
and can kill patients.
And they can cause a lot of pain for families.

Scene 2 [beginning of main body]

Setting:
That night at 9 p.m. I sat on my couch
in my apartment in Hartford
within a mile and a half of that surgical room.
I sat holding my dog, Chester (*character*)
and my uneaten dinner of mac and cheese in front of me,
and I cried.
I couldn't stop for over an hour. (*challenge*)
This was the first time I felt so affected
in medical school.
I felt terrible that one surgeon could put patients in danger by mistreating his team.
I could see this was really important to me. (*lesson*)
I decided I would do better than what I had seen. (*action*)

(Immediate Goal = handle the challenge that moved me to tears. *Challenge* = find a way to do better than the chief surgeon. *At Stake* = become the doctor I want to be and save lives.)

Scene 3

Setting:
The first day back from Thanksgiving.
I sat in Medical School Dean Francis Wells's office (*An action toward a goal, character*)
And asked him,
which classes I could take
that would teach me management skills
to run a medical team well.
She said they didn't have any.
She told me doctors typically learn how to do these things in residency.
Well,
this felt disappointing.
I had seen how residents managed their teams
and I wanted to do way better,
not simply follow tradition.
(I learned) I had to look somewhere else. (*challenge*)
I thought this was ridiculous
because doctors manage so many people in hospitals, clinics,
even in research labs.
(*Immediate Goal* = find training in the medical school. *Challenge* = find classes and get better than the status quo. *At Stake* = become as poor a manager as the examples I've seen and endanger lives.)

Scene 4

Setting:
Well,
I already knew there was a School of Management
at Gryffindor University,

where the MBAs study.
I'd never been there.
I didn't even know a student there.
That night I looked on their website
and I read all about the MD MBA program. (*action toward the goal*)
It was clear that it would add years to my study
and a lot more to my student loans. (*challenge*)
I also learned from my mentor
that doctors are often suspicious of MD MBAs
 because they think the program is for money-hungry people
rather than medical purists. (*lesson and challenge*)
I knew getting an MBA would be a real challenge for several reasons.
(*Immediate Goal* = find training outside Medical School. *Challenge* = weigh the cost. *At Stake* = become a poor manager who hurts people.)

Scene 5

Setting:
The first week in December
I made time to sit in on business classes (*action toward goal*)
in the new Management School building.
As I sat in Prof. Heidi Brooks's class
I discovered terms like "emotional IQ,"
"bottom-up management,"
and "flattened hierarchy."
Later Prof. Cain walked through case studies that discussed
"confirmation bias,"
"overconfidence,"
and "estimation anchoring."
I felt shocked and a little overwhelmed. (*feeling*)
So many ideas were brand new to me.
This was a whole different way of preparing for a career. (*challenge*)
I discovered there was so much I didn't know

and could use right away. *(lesson)*
I saw for certain that there were lessons in that program that I needed
to learn in order to overcome well-known leadership problems. *(lesson)*
I knew the commitment to learn there was important for my career
and maybe all the patients I'm going to serve.
(*Immediate Goal* = see if Management School has helpful classes. *Challenge* = overcoming ignorance. *At Stake* = patients' lives.)

Epilogue

Overarching Lesson:
Now that I'm in my last year of business school,
I've dealt with the challenge
of having very different goals and values than my peers.
I learned business school is a much more practical
and helpful resource for me
then I even imagined
when I first applied to become a doctor.
I love business school
and I see it will make me a much better doctor.

Overarching Bigger Idea:
It is hard
and expensive
and is taking a lot more time
to finish this on top of my medical degree,
but I think it will be worth it.
If I save a few lives
I'll know I did the right thing.
If I help other doctors save lives too,
then I'm certain this is the right investment for me.

Note that in each scene we added, Kelly took a new action toward the goal of learning how to manage a team well. The at stake was the same in each scene because she is moving toward a single big goal of learning management skills even as she faces smaller goals.

You will find more multi-scene stories in the appendix with example stories.

CHAPTER 9

DEVELOPING A DRAFT

DEVELOPING A FIRST DRAFT

As I discussed in the three steps of story development, don't start by writing out your story. This is the mark of a sloppy amateur. Boring stories start and end this way.

If my method is new to you, start by crafting a simple one-scene story. These can be very powerful. Once you are comfortable with this structure, and the response of strangers indicates that you are a compelling storyteller, you can stretch your muscles by complicating the story body with more scenes and sharing more lessons.

FIRST-TIME PRACTICE STEPS

1. *Write down what lesson* from your life you would like an audience to understand. This can be a single lesson or a group of lessons.

Think of yourself as a guide for this audience. What are you sharing with them that they do not know or understand and would like to? If you are telling a personal story, the lesson can simply be how to understand yourself better. You can share a lesson you learned. Getting to know *you* better is the goal of job interviews. But it's not just about landing a job: Investors, volunteers, staff, regulators, and all sorts of people want to know leaders, visionaries, and partners better.

2. *Choose general experiences* that relate to how you learned the lessons. These don't yet have a specific moment identified. For example: I served in the Peace Corps, I interned at a film company, or I was in a bad car wreck in Asia.
Alternative: If you know that you want to share a particular experience, then reverse the first two steps. What is most important is that you have a lesson you are sharing with your story. Listeners remember this as "the point." Everything else should *point* toward it.

3. For the experiences you may decide to use, write out the *essential elements* for each.
For first-time storytellers, this step is more challenging than they expect. My students take an average of forty minutes, with coaching, to list all the elements for a one-scene story. With experience, it may take as little as five minutes. Take the time to do this well. If you don't know what elements make your story compelling, your story will get fat as you try to include everything. Listeners will feel it.

4. In any way that works for you, write out the essential elements and then *plot out the actions you take in the story.*
Include next to them the challenges you faced and the lessons you learned. I use an outline form. Each scene can be moved around, and I can see what a listener must understand at each part of my

story. When my stories have complicated plots, I can see what element each line of the story is moving toward.

5. *Write out the whole story* as if you were speaking it.
I write out my story using one line for each phrase, not each sentence. Some lines have full sentences, some have one word. The spoken stories included in this book are written in this format. I can then mark up this draft easily when refining it later.

6. *Practice with friends* in a space where you can say boring, stupid, and rambling things with no consequences. Then cut out the fat.
I use my living room. Make sure friends know you are working out a new story. The only appropriate friends are those who will tell you truthfully what is boring or worse. They don't need to be story experts. Because most people don't understand how stories work, they won't have the words to tell you exactly what is wrong. They will only have a feeling about it. The same will be true of your final listeners.

Look for those parts that you thought were important but didn't contribute toward an essential element. When I craft stories there is *always* fat to cut. It isn't a bad thing. It is just part of the process.

7. *Practice with different friends* or — even better — acquaintances who will listen for an hour or more.
In this step, I'm memorizing and polishing my delivery. Some editing may occur, but I have a strong sense of my scenes and their order. I serve food and acknowledge my helpers a lot! I can't grow into compelling unless they show me what is working (and what isn't) by their reactions. I will actually schedule shifts of friends— or even just acquaintances—so I can practice standing in front of others for two hours at a time. It is an interactive time where I listen to their questions, see when they laugh, and look them in the eye as I share my heart. I look for the story parts that do these things:

- Cause them to lose interest.
- Confuse them.
- Sound inauthentic.
- Sound forced.
- Can be edited out.

8. *Practice alone* until you are sick of the story.

After the hours invested in the steps above, you should have a story where every word drives your listener forward. You will be confident that the story will create emotional resonance and will communicate the lessons you chose. Now practice this edited and tested version until you're confident you can tell it at any time. When I am preparing a story, I do all this, and then… I practice some more. I do this so that when I tell it in the outside world, I can be emotionally present to the story and never worry about remembering the next word or element.

9. *Refine your story* in the world

Share your stories with anyone you think may like them. Good storytelling develops and matures over time. You will discover what resonates with different sorts of listeners.

Experiment with:

- How much detail to include (probably less than you think).
- In what order to reveal information.
- How many scenes you need.
- How you share the bigger idea.

Look to see:

- When people lean in.
- If there are questions that express interest or confusion.

- Crying.

- Laughter.

- When others share how emotionally moving you are.

- Listeners call others over to hear.

- Listeners summarize your story for others.

- Afterwards others want to give you a hug (really).

Most listeners can't recognize when a story is well-crafted. They simply feel good, connected, and inspired from hearing good stories. So I look to see how listeners react emotionally. They never say, "The at stake drew me in, but the lesson reveal was too predictable from the setup, so the emotional payoff didn't land." Or, "Once I understood the at stake, I got why you committed to the goal, but before that I was bored because I didn't care. You've got to clarify the at stake sooner."

I hope you now know what that feedback means and can offer it to friends who practice their stories with you.

PART FOUR

WISDOM FOR THE FUTURE

CHAPTER 10

PRACTICAL STORYTELLING WISDOM

Now that you know the essential elements for crafting a story and you have a simple structure in which to place them, the next part of this guide will share some lessons important for success. If you're inspired at this point to redraft the personal origin story that you jotted down at the beginning of this book, please do so. The point of the next section is to help you keep a few important ideas in mind to grow as powerful as you can with your stories.

PRACTICE

Good stories take time to craft. Professionals often take days or even months to edit stories so that they sound casual and off-the-cuff. In other words: Don't expect to be able to tell compelling stories immediately after reading a brief guide. A lot of practice is needed to refine skills.

One reason for practicing is that it's hard to know what is compelling when we craft stories by ourselves. When I develop stories, I practice them with friends who understand storytelling.

They help me see what is interesting, boring, and totally unnecessary. You will need the same support. With the Seven Magical Elements and the worksheet included in the appendix, this should be much easier and quicker.

I worked with one finance executive preparing for an important presentation. She had drafted her story before our meeting using principles we'd gone over earlier. When she was telling a story about her son's life-threatening illness, she started crying and had to stop because she was overcome with emotion. She didn't know where her story was going. She was really embarrassed and worried because she was still really bad at telling her story.

I had to remind her that of course she was bad! This was the first time she'd said it out loud. There is nothing else in her life she is professionally good at without practice. This was no different. After practice she'd be comfortable with the emotions revealed and she'd know where the story had to go to fulfill her intention. The same will be true for you.

LEARNING STORYTELLING IN THE WORLD

The best personal stories communicate our growth. They may include important rites of passage (graduation, first kiss, marriage, etc.) or simply lessons learned on the way to becoming ourselves today. When others learn how we matured, they feel closer to us.

Begin at your beginning of you learning to be you. As you encounter new story ideas, *practice* them in the real world. Avoid treating every story as a jewel that must be polished before you share it. Find friends to whom you can tell bad stories that are poorly thought out, poorly structured, and have no feeling. Without an audience, stories are us talking to ourselves. We need others if we are to craft stories well for others. If you and friends read this book, then you will share a common language that will help you all become compelling storytellers.

Stories, conversations, and meetings all happen inside cultures and subcultures. I can't know who you are speaking to, what they expect, or when the right time for you to share will be. So, no matter what I say here, only *you* can know what you should say when you are sharing. The lessons in this book should just help you grow more effective.

STORIES THAT STUN

When choosing which stories to share, you may find that some stories about your formation almost stun you with their power as you are crafting them. Memories will flood back as you think about the specific place, time, and people involved. I watch my clients clasp their chests, clench their fists, and sometimes hide their faces.

There's nothing wrong with this; it just means that you have found something that is deeply meaningful to you. It doesn't mean that you have to share all of it or even that it would necessarily benefit anyone else if you did so. But neither is being stunned a reason to hide that story.

There are those who think leaders should never show deep emotion. I have no idea where that idea comes from. All my leader heroes shared real emotion, vulnerability, and transparency. They inspired generations.

STUCK TALKING SMALL

I'm truly shocked by how many leaders with whom I work share only small goals and small at stakes when they have real bigger goals and at stakes. It is one thing to fear sharing the bigger goals. It is another to be unaware of the bigger goals.

Do you remember the Parable of the Zambian Workers? When I hear many leaders talk about their work all I hear is: "We are working really hard to move this stuff here to over there. We have funding, a talented team, and a track record of success. This is really big stuff we're moving and we are moving a lot of it. We envision moving much more stuff this year over to that area than we did last year. I want people to really understand how much stuff we are moving."

Last year I worked with a nonprofit executive, whom I'll call Lisa, who runs an influential international healthcare program. Part of Lisa's work involves connecting medical thought leaders in the United States with prominent leaders in China. Her program helps bring hard-learned lessons from the best American hospitals to the expanding Chinese healthcare services.

Lisa also oversees delegation visits between China and the United States. She develops international conferences and negotiates relationships complicated by vast language and cultural differences. All of the people involved are proud, accomplished global experts. Lisa also spends a lot of time flying between the United States and China. As you can imagine, her job is challenging. The hours on airplanes and the time zone changes alone take a toll on her.

When I asked her to tell me about her work, she told me about setting up meetings, planning social mixer events for dignitaries, and approaching new funders so the program can grow. All of these activities filled her life.

But I was sure that she doesn't live this challenging life and handle all the headaches and egos involved because her goal is to set up meetings, organize social events, and discuss plans with funders. Those are her small goals. While there is nothing wrong with what Lisa shared, she was stuck talking like the first Zambian worker. Our conversation was about "moving stuff from here to over there."

When our conversation got deeper, she told me how hard it is for Chinese nationals to go to a hospital. Many of them suffer while there, because there is not enough food, training, medicine, or organization. She was moved to tears.

Her real goal is to provide healthcare to at least 1 billion people. She may not achieve it. She is of course a small part in a huge project. But *that is in fact her goal.* What is at stake is the suffering, safety, and lives of more than a generation in China who depend on the Chinese healthcare system.

This may sound obvious now that I write it out here. In our conversation, I was so surprised that Lisa had left that part out. When I brought it up she acknowledged she spent her time talking about small goals and never named the bigger goals, and bigger at stakes, even though those were what inspired her to invest her time, skill, and knowledge.

When she started talking like the third Zambian worker, I got inspired too. I wanted to lean in more and support her growth into the most powerful international healthcare change-maker in the world. I know now that her work is going to affect some portion of 1 billion people. I can't wait to see what happens when others start learning the same thing.

FEAR OF SHARING BIG (AND HONESTLY)

Many leaders are afraid to honestly share their big goals and the big at stakes attached to them.

Lisa, for example, was afraid to tell others the scale of her vision and the at stakes she faces. She, like so many, was afraid that if people heard her talking that big, they would question her credibility. They would think she was a self-important, pie-in-the-sky kind of executive. She could be right: I don't know who she talks to or what they'll think of what she says.

But here is what I do know: Lisa really *is* dedicated to addressing the fear, suffering, and early death risks of more than 1 billion people. That is what motivates her to put up with the travel, egos, and lots (and lots) of paperwork. There must be people who fund her, support her, and depend on her who want to know how deep her passion is and how big her aspirations are. In fact, I cannot imagine a prospective funder or collaborator who would *not* want to know the depth of her passion and the scale of her vision.

Lisa was afraid that if she openly talked about her big goals, people might be disparaging, believing such goals to be unachievable. But if she never shares them, she can never inspire others with her deep passion and vision. She is talking like the first and second Zambian road worker because she is afraid her listeners might dismiss her if she talked like the third one. Ironically, of course, we know exactly which road worker inspires us to get involved.

How do I avoid sounding silly sharing my Bigger Goals and At Stakes? (That is, how do I keep my dignity?)

Anytime we stand up for something really important, there will be somebody who thinks we are silly. I worked as an activist creating and disseminating an international documentary about genocide, and some people thought I was silly. I got a religion degree from a top university in part so that I could help millions of Americans find a way to honor their spirituality outside church traditions, and people tell me I'm ridiculous before they even know what I'm actually doing, for whom, and with whom. If you are leading anything of importance, some people will not like you, and many will think you are silly. That's not so important.

The important question to ask is, "How will the people who matter to our work understand that we are genuine, and in a way that inspires them?" Talking small and hiding a deep passion is not going to do it.

I am not advocating that you open up your deepest soul at every opportunity and in every conversation. But for the people who are going to participate with you and take a risk in some way—don't they deserve to hear your big goals and learn about your big at stakes?

When you read the story about the road workers, I hope you didn't think, "An eighty-four-mile road! How ridiculous! These three guys can't clear eighty-four miles through the bush by themselves. They aren't even road engineers. What makes them think they're ever going to finish a road?"

In the parable, those guys were working as hard as they could. Who knows, maybe they were also working on development grants, negotiating with government officials, and consulting construction contractors. Whatever the case, moving debris also helps a road get made.

Do not depend on the hope of results.

Lisa also feared that some people would laugh at her because she knows that she cannot achieve her grand vision in her lifetime. Fair enough, some will laugh. But what's important is that her listeners will understand that she's working on the next step in the journey. For the Zambian road workers, it is removing the debris in front of them. For Lisa, it is setting up the next delegation, organizing the next meeting, and submitting the next batch of forms.

When sharing our deep passion, it is not important that we achieve the bigger goal. What matters most is that we are working toward it. None of us knows exactly what we will accomplish or not. I never promise my clients specific results. We can make all the plans we want, and all can come undone by something unforeseen. I don't know if they're going to step outside my office and contract Ebola, get a life-changing personal insight, or discover that a loved one is sick and prioritize by canceling all set plans. We have to share that we are doing what we can, with what we have, where we are.

Imagine that I am an ice climber crossing a glacier. I jam my ice pick into the glacier over and over again. When others ask what I'm doing, I'm not afraid to say I'm clearing a passage through this glacier. Some will laugh. Some will ask how long it will take me. I'll say that I don't know. I do know that if I remove the next bit of ice in front of me, eventually there will be a passage. If the at stake is high enough—perhaps we need a path to get medicine to sick children—others may come and join me.

The way glaciers actually disappear is that huge pieces cleave off the face in a single moment. We never know exactly when they will do this, but we know they will. Presumably with enough sun and picking, a break will occur. People want to see that in our own work we are using the tools we have even if results haven't shown up yet. This is *commitment*, doing the work before the results show up.

If the at stake is high enough, and I can inspire others by sharing my goal and demonstrating commitment, then I can build a team to pick the ice. Now I don't look so silly, picking away at the ice by myself. When others see a team picking together, they may get inspired as well and bring in more tools, perhaps power tools. Eventually there will be far more than just me and a hand tool clearing a way through the ice. We can confidently share our bigger goals and at stakes if we do the following:

1. We share our real bigger goals and at stakes for ourselves.
2. We don't mind that some people laugh at us.
3. We are actually working at our own capacity and sharing what that is.

THE HIDDEN DEEPER TRUTH

All too often leaders sit with me and they play cool about how passionate they are about their work. They may *think* that they're showing their real selves, but I know that people who put up with so much struggle, uncertainty, and rejection are motivated by far more than what I usually hear in opening conversations.

Then they ask me, "How can I be more compelling? How can I make our story more interesting? How can I connect with the people we need to create success?"

"You got to start being straight with me," I say. "You have to tell me what you don't want me to know."

To which they often reply, "But I've told you! I've got nothing to hide."

Inevitably there is more. There is a deep longing to make a difference, to do something meaningful, and to offer profound value. But we are all at least a little bit afraid to say it. We are afraid people will think we're silly. We're afraid that we sound naive. We're afraid that we really *are* naive.

It takes a trained and intuitive partner to help us see what we cannot and to acknowledge what we're hiding. But when we do, our resonance and connection with others expands. It took Ed Zogby, an erudite old Jesuit priest and contemplative to help me grow brave enough to talk openly in New York professional circles about the spiritual inspiration of my own work.

There is almost certainly a hidden deeper truth waiting to be shared. When you find it and let it out appropriately, you will almost certainly find others so much more excited to know you.

SHARING STRENGTHS AND WEAKNESSES

Several of my students want to communicate not just their strengths, but also selected weaknesses. For executive directors, it may be what an organization is doing poorly (that's to say, where they need more support) and what it is doing well (and in which they have pride). Business students typically want to share only strengths, but know they may be asked about their weaknesses. I'm often asked how they can share these things with story principles.

In storytelling, as in painting and music, ideas and emotions become clearer with contrast. Seventeenth-century Dutch painter Rembrandt van Rijn is known as a master of light. In his works, dark areas make the light ones shine in contrast. Without the dark, the light would be less interesting. The same is true for storytelling. If you want to share how you are now strong, share when and how you were weak. The same is true for smart and stupid, cautious and reckless, and naive and wise. Ask yourself where can you share contrasts with your listeners.

In the structure we've studied, the *inciting incident is the origin point from which listeners will understand you began to grow in your personal journey.* It is the point with which other story elements (lessons and bigger idea) will contrast.

Strengths

To share a strength, start with a time you were not strong or felt weak and learned how to become strong.

Strength: I can travel light across rural areas without my own vehicle or speaking a local language.

When I was twenty-five years old, my Peace Corps trainer showed us a dot on a map on the wall of our training classroom. This was a village in northern Luapula Province, Zambia, to which we would hitchhike that week, he said. He also told us that we could take only what could perch on our laps, and that the journey would take three days each way.

I felt nervous. I didn't yet speak a local language. I didn't want to get lost, stuck, or hurt. The very idea of hitchhiking for *days* in Africa was way beyond anything I'd tried up to that time.

Fortunately, the trainer added, because this was a "warm-up" trip, we would do this first expedition as a group of four. I wouldn't be alone for this one, although weeks later, I would be. On that first trip, I learned a lot about how to travel with a very small pack, how to find vehicles where there are no public transport options, how to approach strangers, and how to trust that people would help me at every stop. I also learned how *not* to travel, like the time a vehicle drove off with my bag and I didn't know if it would return. After that week, I had learned the skills to hitchhike not only across Zambia but across all of Southern Africa, and by the time I was twenty-seven I had in fact hitchhiked across several African countries and two African national parks. This experience opened so much of the world to me and gave me the opportunity to make friends in places

I had never gone before. I'm still traveling and making friendships that both inspire me and connect me around the world.

When I finish my story, listeners understand how I was formed as a global traveler.

Weaknesses

To share a weakness, I can start with a place where I thought I was strong and I *learned* I am weak. Or I can *learn* how my weakness limits me. Then I can share how I've *learned* to handle this weakness. To stick with a travel theme, I'll share a lesson I learned in Vietnam.

Weakness: I am blind to how poorly I treat people when I'm sick and sleep-deprived.

About a year ago in July, I led a food-and-culture adventure through Vietnam. I've led many adventure trips now and am always thrilled that others trust me with their time and money to explore a new place and discover something enriching. I take pride in prioritizing respectful treatment to all the staff and crew that help us. So many people have to care for us when we are overseas.

In Vietnam, I developed a terrible sinus infection. Breathing was so difficult that I couldn't sleep for three days and my waking hours were painful. Nevertheless, because others were relying on me, I still had to coordinate drivers, vehicle transfers, and food stops. As you can imagine, it was a challenge. I thought I did a pretty good job.

But weeks later on a train through central Thailand, after the group tour ended, my good friend Ming-Yee, who has traveled with me in four countries, told me that she and others were upset with how rude I had been to our bus driver in Da Nang. She knew I was sick and hadn't slept, and she knew how I usually treat support staff, so she saw it as unusual, but not everyone in our group had such long experience with me.

I was mortified. I had had no idea. In that conversation, I learned that when I'm sick and don't get enough sleep, I lose perspective on how well I'm treating people, especially people who are taking care of me and keeping me safe, including our drivers, guides, translators, and administrators. I also learned that I upset the very people who travel the world with me because I'm blind to how I'm behaving. This experience taught me that, at least when I'm sick, and maybe all the time, I need to ask trusted friends to tell me when and if I treat staff rudely, because I don't trust myself to notice it on my own. I need to create a safe relationship where friends feel comfortable calling me out. When they call me out, I need to address whatever needs attention so I don't act like a person I'm embarrassed to be and my poor staff can get the respect they deserve.

General Rule: To share a strength or weakness about ourselves in a story, it is more dramatic to share a point of sharp contrast.

If you want to share how you are good at leadership, then tell a story where you were scared to lead, your ideas failed, or you were abandoned by your own team. You can start with a moment when you realized that you didn't have all the necessary skills. Then you can tell us what actions you took, what challenges you faced, and *what you learned*. Listeners will understand how you have grown in leadership and are better formed.

If you want to share what is a weakness, then share a time when you thought your plan would work and then how challenges taught you that you were wrong. Share what you *learned* now that helps you see that weakness more clearly. Share how you handle this and how it will affect others. There is a lot of emotional appeal in someone sharing how they truly learned they were a failure.

YOUR LIFE'S BIGGER IDEA

It used to surprise me that, within an hour of sharing their own stories, my clients almost always started crying. I came to realize that it was because they were so moved when they understood their own stories clearly. They saw what and who was important to them, what formed them, and what implications their stories had for their own futures. They could see who they wanted to affect and how important it was to them. They could see their life's *bigger idea*. Said another way, they saw the motivating generosity of their lives.

Our stories are so much more than cute, entertaining party tricks. They are informative, dear, and formative. If you notice that your story is bringing up deep emotions and reconsiderations about what you want to say, this is wonderful! It is part of the process of maturing when we start sharing honestly how we are formed.

CHAPTER 11

WARNINGS ON LEADERSHIP STORYTELLING

DATA AND STORIES

Avoid conflating data and stories. When people need data, and that is what they want, give them data. Breaking into a story at an inappropriate time won't help them (or you).

We first discussed data in the "Seven Magical Elements" section. If you recall, we defined data as "stuff you learn how to do or knowledge you gain." Data is important, but it's typically not emotionally resonant. (If you do not remember this, please go back to that section and reread it. It is very important!)

Sometimes when we share data, others can make a story with it. For example, if I share statistics about budget cuts in California mental health services and the subsequent increase in homelessness, a quick story may pop into the head of my listeners. That story may generate feelings, even though all I shared was numerical data.

When we craft our stories, it's important to be clear about what we are sharing and with what intent. If we get into the habit of sharing a story when others want data or vice versa, then we come across as incompetent and unprepared. Others wonder, "Why aren't you simply giving me an answer?"

NOTHING WORKS ALL THE TIME

Sometimes when you tell a story to share a lesson learned, you'll realize that your listeners do *not* take away the same lesson that you learned, or even agree with you about the lesson you *should* have learned. If you tell stories widely, this is inevitable. The academic term for this is *resistant reading*.

We discussed resistant reading early on when I introduced you to the Four Personal Story Rules. The fourth lesson is to remember that your experience and lessons are *yours*.

Stories will not get the "correct" emotional resonance or reveal the "correct" emotional truth that you want every time, nor will they always create the right connection between you and your listeners. Stories simply allow you to achieve emotional resonance and connection more often and more powerfully than mere data can.

This is one reason to focus on offering our lessons humbly and generously. We should *invite* others to pick up our lessons if they so choose. When others reject our lesson (or point), we can then examine how we can emphasize one or another element, or de-emphasize something else, to make our lesson stand out more clearly. Were we clear about the challenge and goal? About what was at stake? About who else was impacted? Even if you share all the elements clearly, remember that not all people will respond as you did, and that is to be expected.

Different listeners will take away different insights. They may even get a *better*, more powerful, and more inspiring lesson. As long as you know this, you won't be surprised when it happens, and you will avoid telling listeners they got it "wrong." They got what you told them, and they interpreted it in the way that they did. You may have told the wrong story for them, and that in itself may teach an important lesson to you.

Example: The Art Gallery Entrepreneur

As an example, I once met with a twenty-something self-described entrepreneur in Oakland. He told me a story about creating a successful art gallery in downtown Oakland. Knowing a little about the difficulties facing any art gallery, I was surprised to hear it. He told me about renting a cheap storefront and inviting artist friends to fill it with art work. I said that his story sounded remarkable. He said with pride, "Yeah, it's amazing it worked."

As I heard more about his art gallery story, I realized that while they had rented a storefront and filled it with works by local artists, he and his friends hadn't marketed the gallery, and made meaningful sales only one night a month thanks to the foot traffic from a monthly street festival. They had never sold enough to cover their expenses, much less make the project financially sustainable. When they decided that they didn't want to continue losing money, they simply closed the gallery. This wasn't an art gallery "success" by any standard I'd consider. I don't know what he considers a success. Was it that he could afford to spend money on a whimsical project in an available commercial space?

I suspect that he shared this story to show me how industrious, brave, and successful he is at a very young age. What I heard is that he is a naive playboy. He and his friends were able and willing to spend money on fun projects in poor neighborhoods without concern for financial return, sustainability, interest in arts organizations success practices, or cultural relevance to the community. Moreover, he considers such whimsical projects success achievements for himself.

Now, I have to admit that I'm a particular kind of listener. I was a working filmmaker in and among New York artists and cultural institutions, I formerly advised museum directors, and I still advise humanitarian organizations working desperately to remain sustainable and relevant. A different audience might have a different response and take away a different lesson.

Example: The Martial Arts Master

Last year I worked with a martial arts master, whom I'll call John, whose inner-city studio cannot serve all the young people who seek him out. After years of success working with kids from poor neighborhoods, John wanted to expand his program to take kids to Asia, introduce them to a new culture, and give them a transforming life experience. John came to me for help in building support for this new program.

John told me a story about one of his former students returning to the studio as a grown man and, standing with him in the studio's courtyard, sharing that John's attention, discipline, and shared life lessons had changed the former student's whole life. That former student credits all of his adult success, and the person he is proud to be, to the relationship he experienced with John. From that conversation, John newly saw that his work was about much more than teaching discipline, self-control, and combat techniques. He then wanted to change his work to grow the most important part, to grow as a resource for saving lives, maturing responsible men, and healing a poor community. After John told me his story, I saw him far differently from how he thought I would. He had shared his story to let me know that *his work changes the lives* of young men who are on dangerous and often criminal paths. But what I heard is that *John has grown into a passionate change-maker*, committed to healing his community and loved by young men who themselves fear sharing their love.

EMOTIONAL MANIPULATION

At one of my lectures, a participant got upset because the story methods I taught "could be used for anything." He was afraid that anyone could use these elements to work for good or for evil. And of course he was right. Someone else that very day noticed how powerful these ideas are and asked about avoiding emotional manipulation.

It is absolutely true that you can manipulate people with these ideas. Marketers do so every day. But I'm asking you to do something more profound here. I want you to *articulate and share your authentic self so that others can be inspired by what you do, why you do it, and how it matters.* I am asking you to do it so they will be moved to join you and make the difference you cannot make alone. This can be with you personally or with an organization you trust and support. This is the opposite of manipulation. *This is authentic invitation.*

For example, if you tell the story of your startup to prospective investors, you could, no doubt, with planning, charting, and deft language, craft a fictional or exaggerated story that generates awe, excitement, and intrigue. But in the long term, unless you can really deliver, you will come to be seen as a manipulative jerk, because that is what you are.

Your brand and your presence will be far more powerful if you use the same tools to craft the *authentic* story of founding your organization, how you envision making a big difference, whom you will serve, and how you will serve them. You will feel more confident when you stump the authentic story across the world, and that confidence will read as truthfulness. *That* is what builds emotional resonance. It is what real heroes do.

EPILOGUE

If you have read from the beginning of this book to this page, you've been exposed to more sophistication on leadership storytelling than most people get in their lifetime. In fact, you've got access to everything I want most students to know to get them to a place where they can represent themselves and their work powerfully and connect emotionally with listeners. Often students say that after working with me they can newly see when and why others sound boring. It's like gaining a new superpower! They felt it before, and now they can name what's missing. You may have discovered after simply reading this book that much of your previous storytelling was boring.

With perhaps your new superpower, please remember that for the most part, other people don't want to know that they're boring (even when they totally are). We all think of ourselves as fairly interesting and capable of captivating for at least ten minutes … until we learn what could make us even more interesting.

Please, do let others who enjoy telling their stories do so. They don't need us smug story experts telling them how boring they are and in what ways. I'm hopeful after our time together you'll help your friends grow proud of their stories, while they help you grow proud of yours.

Let me know if I can help.

APPENDIX A : THE WORKSHEET

This worksheet is a resource to help you start practicing story crafting. Using it, you can create the basic structure or "bones" of a story worth sharing.

After you complete the worksheet, share the story with someone you trust and find out what you don't need (the fat) or what is missing to make the story clear. You may be surprised by how easy it is to make simple stories interesting, even moving. I hope you inspire tears and even a few unexpected hugs.

SIMPLE STORY WORKSHEET

When I'm crafting a story, these are the key questions in my process. When you have all the answers to these questions, your story elements will fall into place.

Collecting Elements

Lesson
What personal lesson do I want to share with my listener?

_____

_____

_____

_____

_____

_____

_____

What experience taught me this lesson?

_____

_____

_____

_____

_____

_____

How did I change or become more mature?

_____

_____

_____

_____

_____

_____

Inciting Incident:
At what moment did I have a particularly strong feeling or thought and make a choice about this? Was there a moment that emotionally moved me or made me cry?

_____

_____

_____

_____

_____

_____

Setting:
Where was I?

_____

_____

_____

_____

_____

_____

_____

When was this?
If I don't remember the date or time, what events happened just before? (birthday, holiday, move, life transition, etc.?)

_____

_____

_____

_____

_____

_____

_____

Characters
Who else was involved in this event that are important to it? What are their names or key descriptors?

_____

_____

_____

_____

_____

_____

_____

Challenge:
After that inciting incident, what new goal did I see, want, or consider?

_____

_____

_____

_____

_____

What prevented me from getting that goal?
Time? Money? Knowledge? Access? Other people? Preparation?

_____

_____

_____

_____

_____

_____

What things did I have to do to overcome those challenges?

_____

_____

_____

_____

_____

At Stake:
What was I trying to create or save?
What would happen if I failed?

_____

_____

_____

_____

_____

Lesson:
What did I learn by overcoming the challenges? (This should obviously overlap, or at least connect, with the lesson you want to share.)

_____

_____

_____

_____

_____

At what point did I learn the lesson?

_____

_____

_____

Bigger Idea:
How is my life and/or other people's lives different because of this story?

_____

_____

_____

Now Put the Elements Together

Setting:
When is the story?
Where is the story?

_____

_____

_____

Characters:
Who is involved?
What are their names? (Or what makes them memorable?)
Who are they to you?
Why are they important?

_____

_____

_____

Inciting Incident:
What happened?
What did you feel and think?
What choice toward a new goal did you set?

_____

_____

_____

At Stake:
What would happen if you weren't able to complete the goal?
What were you trying to create or save?

_____

_____

_____

Challenge:
What was keeping you from completing your goal?
How did you try to overcome the challenge?

_____

_____

_____

Lesson:
What did you learn?
Did you learn to be different?
Did you learn something that is true for you all the time? Is it true for other people as well?

_____

_____

_____

Bigger Idea:
Who did this affect other than you, and how?
Who will this affect other than you, and how?

_____

_____

_____

If you answered all the questions honestly, you should have the makings of a really compelling story. If not, then just like me, you'll simply have to keep practicing with others until you get there. I promise it will come.

APPENDIX B: ADVANCED IDEAS

What I have presented to you up to this point is enough story-crafting wisdom to put you easily in the top 10th percentile of the storytelling leaders I see. My strong recommendation is that you simply practice using the seven elements until you are both comfortable using them and it feels natural. However, I know that in time you will want to grow more, so I am including this appendix with advanced ideas as a bonus. If you are only a beginner in structuring stories, please feel free to skip this section for now. It is here only as a window to a richer storytelling world.

I mentioned earlier that it is not necessary to make stories complicated or long to create an emotional connection or resonance. In fact, simple and powerful is far better than long and weak. When you feel comfortable sharing your stories so that listeners are moved, then you can try using some advanced ideas.

Since this book is a guide for leaders to use stories powerfully, and not about stunning others with deft craft, poetic construction, and nuanced delivery, I'm not going to go deep into these topics. There is no reason to simply drop them all into whatever story you're crafting. That would be like trying to use every musical chord in a song simply because you know they exist.

The cave you fear to enter holds the treasure you seek.

—Joseph Campbell[14]

VULNERABILITY

Vulnerability is a powerful principle to incorporate in your stories and can quickly create a connection in surprising ways. However, I've seen leaders use vulnerability poorly, and then it looks sloppy, manipulative, and distancing (see the section "False Vulnerability," below, for what *not* to do).

Borrowing from Brené Brown's work,[15] vulnerability includes sharing something we are afraid will lead others to reject us if they were to know about it. We are uncertain about how others will react when we share shame. We fear we will be judged negatively. We seek empathy.

I think this works because others identify with sharing shame. We all have our own shame and we can respect others who bravely share their own in the service of creating change. We also believe we are seeing "the real deal" about someone. If he or she shares the shameful parts, then we believe there is honesty worth trusting.

I believe Brown is right in that *we only feel intimately connected with one another when we share vulnerabilities.* Because of this, sharing vulnerability at some point is a requirement for leaders seeking to create connection. Others are honored to be trusted with our shame when we share it in appropriate amounts.

Encouraging leaders to share vulnerability is not advocating that we share anything and everything about which we are ashamed, nor that it should be shared with everyone and at every time. Others must earn the right to hear our darkest shame. If we share too much or too soon, then people will understandably feel disturbed and distance themselves from us. There is a middle ground between no vulnerability and what I call "shame vomiting" that we can explore. I call this middle zone "working vulnerability."

Different audiences have different working vulnerability zones. You will have to experiment with what works. Just know that, when you think about including vulnerability to help make an authentic connection, there are extremes that just don't work.

When we draft our stories, we can include vulnerability by sharing incidents that caused us shame, or times when we noticed (through thought and feeling) that we held onto shameful feelings. Facing our shame can be the challenge element for a scene or a whole multiple-scene story.

As I work with leaders, I've heard shame of all kinds, including these:

Values no longer held.
Project failures.
Inability to resource a vision.
Not growing fast enough.
Growing too fast and then collapsing.
Getting rejected.
Entering a field too late.
Thinking too small.
Lacking creativity early on.
Not being qualified enough.
Going with the crowd.
Rejecting the crowd.
Saying embarrassing things.
Not speaking up.
Speaking up too often, too loudly, too critically, or too forcefully.

To share vulnerability, you have to communicate something that your listener understands to be at least somewhat shameful for you. The test to see if you are actually sharing vulnerability is that you actually feel some fear in sharing it. If you don't, then it is probably not vulnerability.

Brown says that vulnerability always feels like weakness and looks like strength. When we share vulnerability, we almost certainly have to feel a bit weak, but our friends will honestly tell us it looks like strength. It never gets easy. If you think it's easy for you, then you're probably missing the mark.

Since stories are more compelling when they illustrate growth, as we share our vulnerability we can also share how we learned to overcome it so that it no longer controls us. I call this our *maturation*. In this book I share in a story that my first film project was actually inspired by prayer in a contemplative Christian tradition. That is a completely true story, and I assume that some percentage of readers are not going to like it. Some may even feel indignant. They will wonder why I "have" to bring faith into a book about storytelling.

One reason I included this part about my life is that I know that when some readers learn about the truth of how my storytelling career started, they will admire that I put something so vulnerable in plain sight. Some who continue reading will feel more connected to me because they know that I'm presenting myself as my real self. You don't have to like me. You do know who I am.

Choosing Vulnerability to Share

When you want to be sure your stories include some vulnerability but also want to avoid "shame vomiting," there are a few steps that I use to ensure that my choices work. Obviously you have to go through the first two steps in crafting any story, asking:

> *Audience:* Who am I sharing this with?
> *Intention:* What do I want to leave them with?

With leaders, often the answer to the second question is some form of "I want them to feel inspired and committed to join me."

When you think of the people who you want to follow you, you probably want to present a perfectly effective, knowledgeable, and organized version of yourself (if you are normal). But of course you are not perfectly effective, knowledgeable, and organized. None of us is. So given that you and I know that you are not perfectly effective, knowledgeable, and organized, and you think that the audience doesn't know this, answer this question:

What do you not want them to know that is actually true?

The answer includes things about yourself that make you afraid that if they knew them, they might not respect or like you as much. It must be something true. If you're like most of us, there are many things that fit this description.

List them all. Perhaps not every shameful thing about yourself that you want to keep secret in your life, but everything that is true about you leading this work, and that you wish weren't true. Perhaps

- You feel overwhelmed.

- You worry that you have overcommitted.

- You have no idea where you're going to get the funding.

- No one else has made this work.

For many leaders, shameful things include how much they actually care. Really. This is called emotional vulnerability. This includes the fear that if colleagues or funders knew that their motivation includes deep passion going back into their childhood, they'll appear naive and lose respect. I'm not convinced that is true, but this is their fear.

When I discuss this with my clients, they often find something shameful and then tell me "that it isn't relevant." Often they are wrong. They want it to be irrelevant because they don't want to let others know that they know. These are all shameful vulnerabilities I've heard from executive clients:

- I know the organization has treated staff poorly who were fired, has never apologized, and now they are rightfully giving us a bad name in the industry. (regret shame)

- Expanding services is way more about pursuing a personal passion to serve more kids than growing the organization according to a rational and charted plan. (emotional vulnerability)

- All the "priorities" couldn't be handled because there were just too many. (overreach shame)

- I was diagnosed on the Asperger's spectrum when I was young and I know I'm much weaker at making connections on the marketing and sales side than we need right now. (weakness and stigma vulnerability)

- I know my direct report managers can't depend on what I will do and when I'll do it. (undependability shame)

- I'm working to 11 p.m. each night and I'm still worried I'm not doing enough. (overwhelmed shame)

- I've let the board micromanage and haven't taken a stand to establish my authority. (regret shame)

- I'm working so much that I have destroyed my personal relationship and I'm in a very dark place. (lacking balance and control shame)

Who do you want with you?

When you have your list, remember that the thing that you are withholding will still be true whether you share it or not. Then ask yourself: If they knew this, would they actually leave me or would they appreciate that I shared it?

When I ask this question of my clients, they almost always say, "They will appreciate I shared it. They will want to help more." Many times they think their team will respect them more.

But your answer may be, "They will leave me and never talk to me again." You must make your choices in light of this. If they will in fact leave you if they know what is true, then it is important to consider whether you want to depend on people who will leave you if and when they learn the truth. Only you can know what is appropriate vulnerability to share and whether you can handle the risk.

In my experience, most colleagues want to know what we are struggling with as long as we take responsibility for it and meaningfully invite them to help. If they don't want to help, we probably don't want to depend on them.

Sharing a vulnerable truth is always scary, at least the first few times we tell other people. I wish there were another way, but there isn't. So if you're sharing something "vulnerable" and you find it easy to share, it is probably not real vulnerability.

Because it is scary, I always practice with friends who I know are going to stick with me. I practice many times so I know the words will come out.

I've worked with leaders on this in front of groups. I ask them why they are *really* working on making change, and I push them until I get a real answer that isn't concocted to sound smart, organized, and responsible. When their real inspirations are revealed, many times, unexpectedly, tears come. Sometimes the emotions are so strong they can't speak, can't even think straight. A martial arts master cried in front of a room because he was so moved about how much he wanted to change the lives of his inner-city youth students. He certainly didn't expect to do this. It was scary for him, and deeply moving for those of us with him.

The first time you think about some vulnerabilities, the fear, shame, and emotion may overwhelm you. You'll find that after you craft your story and practice it, the raw feelings will become less raw. You will have scenes to share revealing how you learned these vulnerabilities or how they developed. This will allow you to share not just the overwhelming emotion, but a personal journey to which the emotions connect. With practice, those authentic emotions will enrich the story, but they will not control or distract you.

Avoiding Vomiting or Wallowing

On many occasions I have seen people tell stories of a difficult time and hope that, simply by telling it, they will create a connection with their listeners. Perhaps they were once told that it's a good idea to tell stories about their bad times. Unfortunately, this is in fact a recipe for boring listeners and convincing them that you have no point.

Last October, I heard an executive coach I'll call Scott tell a twenty-five-minute story to an audience of fifty people about watching his father succumb to cancer. I still have no idea *why* he was sharing that story. There was no overarching lesson. The only point I got was that "this was really hard for Scott." Later in the training, Scott said something like, "I wanted to be vulnerable in front of you," and therefore he had shared this obviously emotional and hard story. But while he was speaking, I wasn't feeling connected, I felt bored, because I didn't understand his point (nor why he was taking so long to get it out).

I call this kind of story *emotional vomiting or wallowing* (and a story can be both). In either case, the audience doesn't know why the vulnerability is shared—and the speaker often doesn't know either.

Vomiting: Sharing a vulnerable story simply to demonstrate that you can share difficult emotions.

Wallowing: Telling a story that strikes a somber emotional note and stays there.

Avoid Vulnerability Vomiting

The biggest reason Scott's story failed is that it missed an overarching lesson learned (from attending to his father's sickness and death) or a bigger idea (how this experience would affect anyone other than Scott). While his story had several other crafting problems, an epilogue with these two elements would have kept it from feeling like a total wasted twenty-five minutes.

We can avoid vomiting by assuring listeners that we have a reason (a point) in sharing our story. This almost always includes a lesson we learned in the story's journey. For example, Scott shared many scenes that seemed to have no point. He could have selected just a few scenes in which he learned lessons like these:

- I was surprised by how scared I was, even though I always knew death would come.

- I learned that we only had a few weeks left together, and I discovered how precious they were to me.

- I learned that we could share our love for one another much more openly because we knew the end was near.

- I learned that, while he could no longer speak in his final days, simply being near him was important to both of us.

With scene lessons like these the story becomes a formation story about how Scott learned to handle a family death. With a multi-scene story we will need an overarching lesson that's either explicit or implicit, perhaps one of these:

- I learned that time with family is much more precious than I thought before.

- I learned how much family needs one another in the darkest moments.

- I learned I want my children to spend as much time with me as possible while I'm healthy because this time is limited, and when it is gone we can never get it back.

Avoiding Wallowing

Wallowing is when we take our story to a somber place and the emotion remains there. The best stories include emotional changes. We call this *emotional dynamism*. Advanced storytellers think a lot about emotional rhythms, beats, and contrasts. All I want you to understand here is that you don't want to get stuck in somber, or any single note, even happy-joy-joy. It is boring. No one can—or wants to—maintain a single emotion over an endless period of time.

Make sure that you include scenes in which the main characters have a range of different emotional experiences even if the reason for overarching sadness, danger, or fear is still present. Many fundraising appeals and unsophisticated documentary films are wallowing stories: they start by telling us about a bad situation and continue with simply piling on evidence. While the situation may actually be horrible, stories without emotional changes are terrible as well.

Earlier in this book (in the section "A Leadership Story's Three Steps"), I told you about a fundraiser in New York for a Pakistani education program. The speaker got up to make a donation appeal. She began by telling us how dangerous and oppressive Pakistan is for girls and that they have little access to education. She then went on to tell us individual stories of little girls in which each scene started and ended sadly. I'm sure that the stories she told us were true. The situation for girls in much of Pakistan is really dangerous, but she lost my attention because her stories struck only one emotional note. This was in part because she had misunderstood the story-crafting process.

Stories about dark and difficult subjects are not necessarily poor stories; we simply need dynamism. Consider the epic film *Star Wars*. The Empire is a violent, oppressive threat from the film opening to the final act. But the story we follow includes moments of inspiration, delight, success, pride, and humor as well as fear, sadness, and loss. Even in the funniest scenes, we never forget that the genocidal Empire is still a problem for all the heroes involved.

When you share a story about a sad or difficult subject, trust that your listeners can and will understand overarching or contextual threat, concern, and danger. If the fundraiser for girls' educations in Pakistan had included scenes in which the girls felt hopeful, inspired, even protected, we would all have felt more engaged without losing sight of the overarching dangers in their lives.

If scenes with hope and inspiration do not exist, she could have crafted the story to include her own experience of hearing the girls' stories and then having hope and the inspiration that there were teachers, parents, and New York philanthropists who would support the girls in their dreams of getting a safe education and leading long and healthy lives. This would have been far more compelling than the single sad note in which she wallowed.

False Vulnerability

Sometimes leaders will share something that is meant to *look* like vulnerability but isn't. Often the speaker will share something that is framed as shameful but is really something she's proud of.

For example, I once attended a lecture at the University of Southern California where the speaker shared his story about recovering from drug and alcohol addiction. Early in his story he shared about his life clubbing, getting in trouble, and hanging with a fast crowd. The first act was meant to set the context for his eventual work to create a life without alcohol and drug dependence. The problem was that it was obvious from his energetic delivery that he was still proud and a bit nostalgic for those rowdy days. He didn't seem to regret them, and he appeared to enjoy telling us that he had been one of the "cool kids" before his sobriety. As a result, his story's emotional arc didn't work because although he told us about seeking escape from his dependencies, we didn't believe his desperation. His attempt to use vulnerability to create emotional connection failed because he shared no personal risk. Specifically, he never feared that some of us might reject him when we learned he had partied a lot with clubbers.

Of course, since he *did* in fact turn from that life to one of sobriety, there were almost certainly many scenes in his real life experience that he now recalls with shame. And I'm confident there are deeply emotional scenes of desperation, eroded relationships, or squandered opportunities that he could have shared. I'm sure that there were moments where he saw, heard, or learned things that inspired him to invest in sobriety. Had he shared one or more of those moments, we would have felt his vulnerability as authentic. He didn't dig deep enough or take enough risk to accomplish what he wanted.

The lesson here is to take care that what you offer as vulnerability is in fact vulnerability. It is easy and fun to share something safely while pretending that it's otherwise. But it isn't authentic, and your audience will know.

Preparing Vulnerable Stories

Vulnerable stories can and should be prepared and practiced ahead of time. This is not the advice you will always hear. I once heard a famous trainer tell a group that you can't prepare vulnerable stories, you simply have to be in the moment to tell them. It is no surprise that this guy rambles and doesn't know it.

When you craft your story, simply name the unrevealed idea, truth, or lesson that's vulnerable for you. You'll know because it is true, your listeners want to know it, and it is at least a little bit scary to share. Write it down and make sure you include it in at least one of your scenes. If it's an overarching lesson, it may be best to present it in your epilogue. You can even simply tell listeners *why* you are sharing this vulnerable thing so that they know you have intention.

Then practice telling your story in front of trusted friends, including this vulnerable element. Then ask them these questions:

- Did they understand what the vulnerable thing was?

- Did they understand the intention (implicitly or explicitly)?

- Do they see you as stronger of feel more connected now that you have shared it?

THE RULE OF THREE

When we hear stories, our brains like sets of three. I don't know why. If you want to illustrate or emphasize a point, or share examples from a large set, it will sound better if you share them in sets of three.

For example, I worked with one executive who was telling the story of her organization. She told me about a time when a staff member called her because that person had had a bike accident and needed a ride. When the executive got to a point she wanted to emphasize, she said this:

> When I got there
> I could see she had fallen forward on her bike.
> She was bleeding.
> It was bad.
> It was really bad.
> I couldn't believe it."

She obviously wanted to emphasize how bad she thought the sight of blood was. A stronger method is to use the Rule of Three, and share three observations to illustrate the scene:

> When I got there
> I could see she had fallen forward on her bike.
> (1) There was blood on her face,
> (2) on the handle bars,
> and (3) on the pavement.
> I couldn't believe it."

We can use the same Rule of Three if we want to share a few of many incidents in a set. In the example below, a staff person is giving examples of a work environment she left. She wanted us to understand that her boss was a terrible micromanager:

> My boss was a terrible micromanager.
> She would have all kinds of rules

on how I could do my job.
She even observed all my communication
all the time.
She was just terrible.

Here is the same idea communicated using the Rule of Three:

My boss was a terrible micromanager.
For example,
1) she required that I get permission
for each pencil I ordered.
2) She required that I copy her on every email to every one of our
vendors.
And she said
3) I could only make calls that were less than twenty minutes
long.

When wondering how many items to list as examples to make a point, experiment with three and see if you need more. In most cases, you won't. The three-beat feels more satisfying and complete for the listener. But don't trust me: experiment!

HUMOR

Don't tell jokes. *Don't tell jokes.* As a new storyteller, if you wonder whether you should tell a joke in your story: don't. I have seldom seen an inserted joke enrich a compelling story. It usually distracts listeners from what should be a powerful and enriching point. When jokes have been used well, it is always by *very* experienced storytellers who are deft with pacing, hidden meanings, and emotional shifts. If you try to insert jokes without rich experience getting simple stories right first, then it will be like trying to improvise jazz like Wynton Marsalis in your first month of music lessons. It will not go well ... yet.

Many books have been written about humor. Tastes differ widely and work in culturally specific ways. The lowest form of humor is sarcasm and the highest is satire. I'm not going to cover all the forms here. For the purpose of helping your beginning story crafting, I want to introduce two important ideas.

American audiences typically associate humor with surprise. Other cultures do as well, but typically the British appreciate silly humor more than do Americans. This is especially true about people acting outside of their station and class.

For Americans, if we think we know where the story is going and then we are surprised, this shift can be humorous. This is far better than inserting a joke. I use *surprise* by telling stories in such a way that listeners are lulled into predicting the end of a scene or an outcome and then I surprise them.

You can use this principle for using humor in the Rule of Three.

The Humor Rule of Three

The Humor Rule of Three depends on listing three things. These can be anything in a set: thoughts, items, experiences, lessons.... The important trick is that the first item introduces the domain (the sphere of possibilities), the second item establishes a pattern, and then the third item *surprises* by breaking the pattern.

For example.
Each morning I do three things.
1) I shower,
2) I walk my dog,
and
3) I feed a soul-sucking Internet addiction.

When preparing dinner
1) I made sure we had candles,
2) seats for everyone,
3) and enough butter to drown the lobsters
even though they were already dead.

The first two items set up a pattern, lulling listeners into predicting what comes next, and the third breaks the expected form.

To make sure that the surprise element isn't simply a throw-away gag line or joke to get a cheap laugh, you can explain how and why the surprise element is honest. This enriched explanation acknowledges the humorous surprise and invites listeners to understand nuance.

Each morning
I do three things.
1) I shower,
2) I let my dog out to pee, and
3) I feed a soul-sucking internet addiction.
(*enriched explanation*) I know each morning
that this is a time to prepare for the day,
but I don't know how to resist
checking if anyone
is desperately trying to reach me on email.
And then my brain pulls me
to the *New York Times* front page,
and within three minutes of waking,

I'm no longer in my home
with my family,
I'm on the Internet reading about stuff
that I'll do nothing about.

When serving dinner
1) I made sure we had candles,
2) seats for everyone, and
3) enough butter to drown the lobsters
even though they were dead.
(*enriched explanation*) You see, I've learned
that guests like good food,
they like a pleasant room,
and they love butter.
If butter makes everything better,
then I figure
I'll serve lots of it.

Acknowledged Stupidity (a Kind of Self-Deprecating Humor)

The other concept I'll introduce here is what I call *acknowledged stupidity*. This is when we tell a story and we let our listeners know that we now realize that what we did, thought, or felt in the story was not good, wise, effective, smart, or even safe. The audience is invited to join us in rolling their eyes at our past stupid self. This works because we are inviting listeners to join us in our empathy and shame about our former self—an experience we have all had. We share the surprise of what you did in the situation in the story. When you listen to great orators, notice if they are inviting listeners to honestly mock their past selves when audiences laugh.

This is related to self-deprecating humor, but a bit more nuanced. With acknowledged stupidity, the listener is completely aware that you think the choice you made in the real-life story was stupid or at least unwise. The humor comes in them joining you in your newfound wisdom. I use this kind of humor when I tell about getting my first experience at a real movie studio.

> When I was at USC,
> I heard a story about Steven Spielberg.
> The story I heard
> was that he also
> didn't have special skills or
> connections in Hollywood
> or a clue where the on-ramp was
> to become a successful filmmaker.
> So,
> the story was
> that he put on a suit to look older,
> got a briefcase
> to look like he had a job,
> and walked right up to the Universal Studios gate.
> When he got to the gate
> he just acted like he worked there
> and the guard waved him on to the lot.
> when he got on the lot
> he found an empty office
> and made it his.
> and he returned every day
> to "his" office
> right until
> someone figured out he didn't belong there
> and told him to leave.
> But by that time,
> he had built the relationships he needed
> to become a successful filmmaker.
> So,
> I thought,
> if it is good enough for Steven Spielberg,
> It is good enough for me.
> You probably see where this is going.

It is a totally true story.
With all of the wisdom of a twenty-year-old,
I put on a pair of khakis
because that was the style
of young people at studios in those days.
I got a manila envelope,
filled it with my resumes
and wrote "Icon Productions" on it
because I knew Icon was on the Warner lot.
Then I went right up to the Warner Brothers Studios gate,
and when the guard looked at me,
I pointed to the envelope
and said,
"This is for Icon Productions."
Which was true.
I didn't tell him it was full of my resumes
or that they'd never heard of me
or that I was sneaking in.
In fact,
I still can't believe,
as I look back on this
about twenty years later...
that it totally worked.
He waved me onto the lot.
When I passed through that gate
I felt exhilarated.
It was the first time in my life
I had been in a real movie studio
without visiting as a tourist.
I was so close to the people
who I wanted to be.

Then I felt afraid
because I wondered when someone would figure out
that I didn't belong there.
So I went into every production company I could find

and I handed over a resume
and said in so many words,
"Can I work here?"
Well, at that time,
Kara Francis ran the story department at New Regency
Productions.
She was so impressed
that I snuck onto the lot,
went into offices that didn't want me
and handed out resumes
that no one wanted,
that she said
you can totally work here...

for free...

as an intern.

And that is how I got my first experience
at a real movie studio.

You may not think this story is hilarious. What I hope you can get from the transcription is that I know as the teller that this was kind of an unbelievable and silly way to start a career. When the audience joins me, they often laugh. They especially laugh when the surprise is revealed that I got an invitation to work for free.

The scene I share about sneaking onto the Warner lot is part of a bigger story. It still works as a scene because there is change (I get my first studio internship) and I learn something (I can get experience by taking risks and passing out unwanted resumes). There is no bigger idea in this scene because that element comes later after several other scenes. Without it, you can feel that this story is perhaps cute but emotionally unsatisfying. It lacks real emotional resonance or drama. The at stake is my dream of becoming a filmmaker, but it is a selfish goal and too low an at stake to create real connection with my listeners.

If you want to use the acknowledged stupidity principle, you must share experiences where you now see you were silly, naive, or stupid, and let your audience know that you understand that is so. When you include a good at stake, lesson learned, and bigger idea, the story will work far better than just sharing a list of stupid things you did when you were younger.

AUTHENTIC EMOTION

Two years ago a workshop participant I'll call Veronica told me that she was afraid to tell the story about her inspiration to work in hospital management, because she was sure that she would start to cry. I told her that this would be the best-case scenario.

I don't know who your listeners are and what they like, so I can't know if crying in front of them is a good idea. Unfortunately, how women and men are perceived when we cry is very different. I wish I could do something about this or have clairvoyance about when is the best time to show deep emotion.

In every experience I've had in which someone's personal story moved them to tears because of their passion, it had a galvanizing effect on the listeners. No one could look away. I'm not talking about tears from sadness, victimhood, or pain by itself. I'm talking about tears from personal commitment, hope, and lessons learned.

Earlier in the guide I told you how Dr. Kelly wants to save lives by running her surgical teams well. I know the experiences that inspired her and moved her to tears. I cannot even imagine how connected I would feel to my doctor if she told me about how much she is committed to managing her team well and I saw tears of commitment run down her face.

Someone in your life has probably told you to hide your tears. Maybe they were right. Maybe they know something I don't know about your life. But they probably haven't distinguished between the tears of fear and the kind that come from inspiration, passion, and commitment. They may not know how connected and trusting a team feels when they see that their leader is genuine, a person who cares about making a difference far more than about looking good doing it.

I invite my listeners to be with me in my emotion. I've seen that when many story tellers experience deep and uncontrollable emotions, they will 1) turn away, 2) apologize, and 3) press their lips together to show a strong face. These actions do not invite listeners to join in and connect to the emotion. On the contrary, the message I get when I see this is, "I don't trust you to share or empathize with my most deep feelings and the things I care most about."

When you tell stories that are important to you and have shaped your whole life, honest, powerful stories will tap into honest, powerful emotion. Your listeners, who want to know you better, want to feel those emotions too. They will trust you more because you shared those emotions, as long as the emotions are real and related to the subject at hand.

When my overwhelming emotions come and I can't continue smoothly, I simply pause. I trust that my listeners notice that I'm deeply moved. I trust that they can handle a pause. I don't apologize. I don't turn away. When the emotion has settled a bit, I simply continue. Sometimes I'll acknowledge what happened so they know that I'm okay with the feelings. I'll say, "I'm deeply moved by this."

You have probably already figured out that when we share authentic emotion, we are sharing a kind of vulnerability. We may fear that someone in the room will judge us and reject us because we're crying. The irony of learned wisdom is that it is exactly this vulnerability that connects others with us emotionally.

Being Present to the Emotion

It is true that vulnerable stories work best when we are emotionally present to their importance to us as we tell them. Said differently, we allow the emotions to be present as we speak.

This can happen no matter how much you have crafted ahead of time or practiced. I practice so much that every word is ingrained and I'm often sick of the story. Then I practice at least two more times. After I've done this, all the words come right to me when I tell the story. I never worry about remembering. This confidence then gives me freedom to feel the emotions that come as I share. I'm not distracted by fear that I won't remember what comes next. I can look listeners directly in the eye and know I will finish a story that will move both of us.

It is possible that, after telling the same story many times, not only do we memorize it, but we can also lose emotional connection with it. This has happened to me. It is an opportunity to be like stage actors reciting the same lines night after night. When we start sharing an emotional story, go slow and allow yourself to relive the story. Be present with the scenes, the lessons, and the conviction the story inspires in you. If you do this honestly and patiently, the emotional connection will return.

For example, I have worked with an activist—I'll call her Michelle—who is creating a community network for children of same-sex couples. There are many reasons that make her work so valuable. She can tell you all about them. But what really inspired Michelle was a series of vulnerable experiences.

When she was about eleven years old, growing up in a conservative state, she saw the first of many television ads calling for political action to abolish families with same-sex parents, like hers. She was shocked and afraid when she saw the first ad and grew more afraid over the following months. She grew to be ashamed of her own family. She lied about her parents outside her home. She feared that school friends would abandon her if they knew her family actually had two fathers. She even distanced herself from her fathers because of the shame.

Now that she is older, she has far more shame about how she treated her fathers, how much she dishonored them and their commitment to raise her as a strong and educated young woman. She is also embarrassed by the narrow-minded ideas she held as a young teenager about what a "real" family looks like. The fear she felt as a girl still pains her. When she shared her story and felt the fear, shame, and regret, she cried in front of our group of thirty. She could not stop her tears. She apologized many times for her crying. I didn't ask her to either apologize or stop. In fact, her emotional truth and bravery was the best example of sharing authentic vulnerability that we saw all evening.

She didn't want us to know about how she treated her family when she was ashamed of them. In other words, she is now ashamed of what she did then and who she was. She almost certainly intended to hide that when she stepped up to work with me. She wanted to avoid the emotional exposure. But by revealing both the shame and emotion, she shared vulnerability, and the room was riveted. She felt weak, embarrassed, and stupid, but we saw her as brave, authentic, and inspiring. If she had asked me to help her build this network, I would have said yes on the spot. Her vulnerability showed me that she was real, and I—and the rest of her audience—believed that her goal is to make others feel safe, welcome, and whole.

Because this was the first time in her life that she shared the story of her shame and fear with a group, her tears came uncontrollably. She had to stop talking for several minutes. In time, after she crafts her story into scenes, distinguishes the lessons that formed her as an activist, and practices her delivery, the emotions will become less raw and more controllable. In her best moments, she will be present again to the meaningfulness of her story and some of those authentic emotions will surface. Her listeners will feel this and she will create connection. We knew it was real vulnerability, and not something superficial and manipulative, because we could feel how scary it was for her to share it the first time.

Emotional Limits

It is *not* true that talking about anything that will bring up emotion is a good idea. That's what I call emotional vomiting. It is usually manipulative and slimy, and it looks desperate. Stories are only helpful if you share something that is pertinent to your listeners.

This almost always involves sharing something that we learned that formed us in some way that helps them understand us and our relevance to them. This can include learning how much we care about something.

This book gives you permission to pause when big, authentic emotions well up. Wait for the emotion to subside. Acknowledge the emotion to your listeners and keep moving forward with your stories. Most of the time your audience will respect you more for it and consider you one of the most interesting people they know.

FLASHBACKS

A *flashback* is a tool that breaks up the story timeline in such a way that a scene takes place not after, but before—maybe years before—the previous scene. You have often seen this in films and television. Flashbacks are typically used for one of two reasons:

1. The importance of a story is revealed later in the timeline. So we introduce the scene that explains the at stake or significance, then we flash back (break the timeline) to tell the story that leads up to the moment that makes the importance clear. Typically the scene later in time sparks a question like, "How did they get here?" or "How did they wind up in this situation?"

2. In order to explain an element in a story timeline, we must flash back to an earlier time to explain something to the listener.

> ### *The Lunch Example:*
> I remember in the spring of 2012
> I would sit in the University Commons Dining Hall twice a week
> for lunch
> wondering if someone would join me.
> Sometimes no one did
> and so I'd sit alone
> in a giant dining hall about a block long
> eating by myself.
> Surrounded by college students
> enjoying a break in the day
> and youth.
> I actually learned
> that was one of the most important things I did.
> I'm not kidding.
>
> (*Timeline break*)
> You see, in my first semester at camups,
> my friend Scott Sherman was invited to teach
> the first social entrepreneurism course at University.

After more than sixty students competed
for the eighteen spots,
he asked me to join him.
He knew about my genocide education work,
nonfiction media,
and fundraising experience.
I spent that first semester getting to know
some of the most generously motivated,
globally thinking,
and unafraid students at campus.
It was quite a welcome.

When the semester ended,
Scott flew back to Los Angeles,
but in some ways the class,
really now a community,
didn't end.
Students like Elizabeth and Alison
told me they wanted a chance to still connect,
learn,
and share support.

So we set up a weekly lunch
that any of us could join.
In the beginning it was exciting to get back together.
Then people got "busy."
Some asked if they could bring friends,
and so our ranks expanded
and a group of regulars formed.
Eventually the Social Entrepreneur students all graduated.
But the regular lunch was attended by friends
and friends of friends
who became my friends, too.

But papers
and research

and classes
get in the way.
I didn't always know if anyone would join me.
There were many times when it was just me
and I wondered if I was silly—
Maybe a loser
sitting at a lunch
no one wanted to join.

But then a surprising thing would happen.
Sometimes one person would join me.
Just one.
And we would share
an unplanned lunch for two.
And those conversations would grow the deepest.
Without the distraction
and posturing for a group
we talked about hurts
and questions of meaning
and things that really weren't working.
Those conversations often went more than two hours.

I could see by the length of the conversation,
the deep pauses,
and sometimes the tears,
that these were the most important conversations.
I learned that knowing lots of people
was not actually better
for what I wanted to do,
for who I wanted to be.
For connection,
learning,
and support

I learned that when no one showed up to our lunch
it simply meant that at any moment

it could be the best lunch.
I learned it was important that I was available.
I was being the resource,
sitting alone,
that could be
the exact kind of lunch
someone is looking for.

SHAPE-SHIFTING CHALLENGE

There are many ways to think of shape-shifting in storytelling. For the purposes of this guide, I want to introduce you to a very specific kind of shape-shifting. A *shape-shifting challenge* appears to change as you progress on your journey. This does not necessarily mean your challenge was blue and is now orange, or had two arms and later has four. It simply means that the challenge you thought you were facing in the beginning is different from the one you understand at the end. Often in films we see a progression from small to big or big to small. For example:

Small to big:
Act 1: We are investigating an office break-in and robbery.
Act 2: We discover that this is a covert operation by a conspiracy to discredit Daniel Ellsberg.
Act 3: This is a story about unseating a corrupt president who is using hired thugs to violate the Constitution.

Big to small:
Act 1: We arrive as a fully armed military outfit to rescue colonists and restore a power plant on a far-off planet.
Act 2: We discover that the colonists are dead and the planet will soon explode.
Act 3: We work to save one little girl and get off the planet in one ship.

An example of a shape-shifting challenge in a personal story:

1. I arrive in my village to help with water sanitation to save lives. The challenge appears to be fighting ignorance on how to protect village people from communicable pathogens.
2. I learn that villagers can't afford soap and must burn trees (leading to deforestation) to boil water. *The challenge appears to be village economic poverty.*

3. I learn that villagers can't get fair prices for crops or supplies because infrastructure investments have been stolen by provincial officials. The officials also kidnap and beat any villager who speaks up against the stealing. *The challenge appears to be local corruption.*

4. I learn that local officials will never be prosecuted or imprisoned no matter what evidence is presented because the ruling political party will protect its own and all power is maintained by corrupt favors. *The challenge is the national political structure, a nominal democracy.*

If we tell scenes that explain each of the progressions above, listeners will see that the shape-shifting challenge changes into something far bigger at the end than it had seemed at the beginning. A changing challenge can be far more interesting than a static one.

RELUCTANT HERO

The *reluctant hero* trope is one in which the story hero originally refuses an (explicit or implied) opportunity to pursue the story's goal. She does so because she has fears, concerns, other priorities, or simply doesn't want the expected fruits of success. Then an inciting event occurs that causes her to commit to (choose) the story goal and face the necessary challenges. Often the inciting incident heightens the personal at stake for the heroine. The inciting incident may confront the heroine about her true values and who she believes herself to be in the world. This is a trope used in just about every Disney film. Take two minutes here: I'm sure you can think of at least three stories you love starring a reluctant hero.

When a character initially refuses to go on the journey, we understand why she doesn't want to go. When she then accepts, we have already witnessed a measure of internal growth on her internal journey. We also get a sense that she is really committed because she began the journey only after overcoming the concerns that held her back. Here is an example of a reluctant hero opening to a longer origin story I know about a labor activist.

> When I was in my twenties,
> I was a young artist in New York City.
> I waited tables before my work could pay me enough
> to live in the city.
> The first time I walked into Café Quatrefoil
> I was intimidated by its beauty.
> It was then and perhaps still is among the highest grossing restaurants
> in the most competitive restaurant market in the world.
> Maybe that ever was.
> The restaurant sits right on Broadway
> on the Upper West Side,
> Across from the Metropolitan Opera,
> the American Ballet Theater,

the New York Philharmonic,
and a music school
called Julliard.
Their audiences were our guests.
I was the worst waiter the Cafe never fired.
Among many things,
I learned that the beauty and glamour of the restaurant
was built on the backs of people who did not have
options
and were abused.
Like Baru,
a Bengali immigrant
who was raising a family in Queens
with the portion of my tips he got;

Like José,
the Ecuadoran immigrant
who made all the coffees for the 300-seat restaurant
fourteen hours a day
with no breaks.
He still owed thousands and thousands of dollars to the snakehead
who snuck him into the country.

Like Jenny, who,
honest to goodness,
rented the women's bathroom from the restaurant,
and with no pay or provided budget
stocked it with fragrances,
mouthwash, and candy,
handed towels to guests,
and made a living off the tips they gave her.

That spring I quit my table-waiting job
so I could work full time as an artist.
A scant few weeks after I left
I found a newspaper article

that reported that workers from one of our sister restaurants
in the $60 million restaurant group
were suing the management for wage and labor violations.
Simply put,
for stealing money from workers.
But that was not the most interesting part.
The more interesting part
was that the company was suing the workers for defamation.
Simply put,
for lying about what was going on in the restaurant.
Now,
I had just completed two and a half years,
becoming a senior server in the flagship restaurant,
and I knew that every night before I left
the management illegally required me
to hand over a portion of my cash tips to managers.
We never saw it entered into the company computers.
I had worked numerous fourteen-hour shifts without a break.
I knew of numerous other labor violations.
I knew the workers were telling the truth.
So I sought out the nonprofit organization that was supporting
and advising the workers
in their stand for justice.

It was called the Restaurant Opportunities Center.
I made an appointment with the executive director,
Anjali Kade.
Anjali is an interesting character.
She spent years getting law and government degrees from NYU and
Columbia.
But she had never worked a single day in a restaurant.
I sat in her Tribeca office
and we had a conversation that would change both our lives.
She shared that she was looking for someone to organize the other
workers
in the $60 million company

to join the fight for their rights.
She asked me
if I would be that person.
I hesitated.
I explained that I had benefited from the system.
I thought it was at least unfair for me to leave it
and then cry foul.
She asked me to do it not for myself but for Baru.
And José.
And Jenny.

This is when I understood:
Unlike Baru and José,
I had the education to understand the law,
I had the language to articulate our concerns and vision,
I had the citizenship to confidently go into courtrooms
and talk to judges
without fear of deportation.

Because I had left the restaurant,
I had the time flexibility to work on the issues.

Unlike Anjali,
I had years of experience waiting tables.
I had credibility with the workers.
They knew I had no political agenda.
I wasn't building a law career.
And they knew for certain
that I was no corporate spy.

Very soon after,
my former Cafe colleague Sam
walked into the Starbucks at Astor Place downtown.
I was waiting for him there
because it was a place of his choosing
and a time of his choosing,

so he would be confident
the company wasn't spying on him.
He sat down
and I had my first conversation
as a secret labor organizer in New York City.

SUDDEN LATE REVEAL

The *sudden reveal* is a trope by which we reveal information late in the story that reframes or reinterprets what we learned earlier. This can be a lot of fun for listeners because they get to think back about what they thought about the story and see it in a new light.

A sudden reveal will be ineffective if the storyteller makes it obvious there is an upcoming reveal that will make the first part of the story relevant. The challenge in using this trope is to tell the story in such a way that listeners (even trained storywriters) are surprised by the reveal and take delight in it. Obviously, this takes skill and craft: don't depend on this until you've really mastered the basic elements.

Here's an example of a story with a reveal that I heard at a fundraising event for a music performance program. The program's executive director shared it, hoping that he would inspire us with his experience and help us understand the difference that an introduction to music performance could make for a young artist. I have masked some identifying details, and I've edited the story slightly to make it work better. The arc of the story and the lesson remain as it was told to me:

> In 1969, I was seventeen years old and needed a job.
> My dad knew the manager of the Raven Music Club.
> With a call from my father,
> he hired me to be a gopher.
> I think they called me a production assistant.
> I remember that first day I was hauling gear.
> I took tickets.
> I was trying to figure out how the place worked.
> At one point I was standing backstage in a hallway
> and one of the musicians was standing at the green room door.
> He said,
> "Hey, come on in, kid."
> So I went inside,

It was the first time I got to see musicians warm up,
joke around like old friends do,
and just chill out
as artists do before a performance.
At seventeen it was really cool to be around real musicians.
I was just thrilled be there.
It seemed to me that they came
from a foreign world I wanted to be a part of.
That guy who invited me into the green room
was
Bob Dylan.
I guess he saw a young kid
trying to be cool
and he invited me into his world,
a world I fantasized about.
He and that job changed my life.
That day I was hooked on the music industry
and I've spent my whole life there since.
I'm hopeful this program will give these kids
the experiences,
skills,
and joy
I got when I was just a kid.
This is why we're creating this.

Two things are true about this sudden reveal. First, we reinterpret the excitement level for his teenage self when we discover he was invited to hang out with Bob Dylan instead of a no-name local artist. Second, try re-reading the story but change the opening of the key scene: " At one point I was standing backstage in the hallway, and Bob Dylan was standing at the green room door." Do you see how much less effective that version of the story feels? By delaying the reveal, we give the listener a bit of surprise and joy.

COLLECTING TOKENS

In ancient myths, wise elders often give tools or wisdom to heroes that help them on their journey. We call these *tokens*. At the time the gift is made, the hero often does not understand how the tool or wisdom will help, or even whether it will be of any use at all. But in the course of the journey the tool's value is revealed. It may even save the hero's life. Here are some tokens you may know:

1. Cinderella's glass slippers are given by her fairy godmother in the Cinderella fairy tale.
2. Luke Skywalker's light saber is given by Obi-Wan Kenobi in *Star Wars.*
3. Frodo's mithril armor is given by Bilbo Baggins in *The Lord of the Rings.*

When you craft your stories, there may be pieces of wisdom or tools that appear to have little value when you get them from someone, but later in your journey you discover they have great value, maybe even so much value that they are key to your success or formation.

A common way to incorporate this trope is to mention early in the story a piece of folksy or seemingly dated wisdom about how the world works from someone in your family, who doesn't understand much, you believe, about how the world works, or at least not about how *your* world works. Then when you face your challenge, you recall the seemingly useless or trite wisdom. In a different place and time, you now understand its power and truth. This insight helps you overcome the challenge in front of you and mature into someone far wiser than before.

Token as Symbol

A token can be any object that represents a value set or a memory that is important to you. When you see or remember the object, it reminds you of something that helps you overcome a challenge or mature.

An example of symbol token: (this one is fiction)
Summer Camp Story Scene List

1. Mom helping me pack my bag. Shirts, underwear, socks, swim shorts, sunscreen, and a pocket knife.
2. Father dropping me off at the bus with lots of kids I don't know.
3. Meeting kids in my cabin filled with fear and loneliness.
4. Watching other kids pick on Christopher.
5. Joining kids picking on Christopher to fit in and keep friends.
6. Experiencing Tokens as value reminders:

   - Holding the pocket knife mom gave me.

   - Remembering how embarrassed she would be if she saw me teasing Christopher.

   - Pulling out the granola bars Dad gave me for the bus ride.

   - Remembering how he always stays with the last person on any hike or swim and helps them the whole way.

   - Sitting with Christopher at lunch and learning to be a person who is principled and strong rather than mean and a coward.

GETTING HELP FROM A WIZENED GUIDE

In great epics, the hero never accomplishes his journey alone. A *wizened guide* offers wisdom, tools, and direction, and maybe even saves our hero when he seems about to fail. These wizened guides give us a sense that the hero stands in a tradition of wisdom passed from one generation to the next, and that he is part of a larger community that roots for his success. Earlier, I wrote about elders passing on tokens. These can be tools, learned wisdom, or symbols. Wizened guides are great characters for passing on tokens that help you on your journey.

Virtually every epic story you have ever heard includes wizened elders helping a hero through challenges. I'll just list a few so you can recognize the trope. Then I encourage you to look at other stories you like; you'll find a lot of wizened elders:

1. Glinda the Good Witch to Dorothy in *The Wizard of Oz.*
2. Dumbledore to Harry Potter in the *Harry Potter* series.
3. Prof. Digory Kirke to Lucy in *The Lion, the Witch, and the Wardrobe.*

A wizened guide can be anyone who seems to have more experience or knowledge than you do. It isn't important that they have exact knowledge of your challenge at hand. For example, in *Star Wars*, Obi-Wan does not have actual experience shooting torpedoes into an exhaust vent on the Death Star. He does have experience resisting the forces of the Dark Side and accomplishing seemingly impossible tasks. Though his experience is different, it guides Luke Skywalker to become a more effective and mature man.

Surely you have people in your own life who helped you on your formation journey as a person, leader, entrepreneur, or activist by guiding you, warning you, or supporting you in important ways.

You already know that good stories are about a character facing challenges on the way towards a goal. Tell your listeners how wizened elders helped you in ways that made a big difference. By doing so, you will give us a sense of three things:

1. You are part of a community.
2. You stand in a tradition.
3. You understand that others are important in your formation, along with your own choices.

GOING TO A FOREIGN (MAGICAL) LAND

With this trope the heroine goes to a *foreign land* where the rules of her homeland no longer apply. While she visits this foreign land, she learns lessons she will use on her return. The foreign land is also referred to as a *magical land* because the rules that limit possibilities at home no longer apply in the magical land.

The foreign lands in your stories do not have to be actual foreign countries or magical realms. They can simply be a place where the rules are different. These rules can be cultural, civic, or moral. The foreign land can simply be a different community or, as we say, a different tribe. A tribe is simply a group of people with similar values, interests, and rituals.

Peace Corps, war, college, and travel stories are often by definition stories that use a foreign land trope. In these stories, heroes learn something in a place with new rules and bring that wisdom (maturation) home. For example, in Dr. Kelly's story about becoming a more effective surgeon, she travels to the foreign land (tribe) of business school to learn lessons she will bring back to her medical tribe.

This is a fairly easy trope to use. When your inciting incident inspires a new goal, your story can take you to another tribe where an experience teaches a lesson you will bring back to your tribe from the story's beginning.

NEW TOOLS

The *new tool* trope is one in which a hero learns that the tools he has been using to overcome obstacles and achieve his goal will not, in fact, suffice. He learns to use new tools that he hasn't used or relied on before. This trope can be very satisfying for a listener: we get to see the hero's maturation from ineffective to a more mature, effective self.

My favorite example of this trope is in the climax of *Star Wars*. Luke Skywalker flies his X-wing fighter down a fortified trench on the Death Star. He is trying to drop torpedoes into a small vulnerable exhaust vent using his computer guidance system. At the last moment, he hears a mystical voice from his seemingly dead elder, Obi-Wan Kenobi. Obi-wan says, "Use the force, Luke." Luke turns off the targeting computer system. It literally pulls away from him. He then completes the mission by using the force (a mystical strength). This scene is satisfying in part because we see Luke's maturation when he rejects the instructions and tools of the non-mystical leaders who planned the mission. He chooses to use, for the first time, the tool taught to him on this adventure that he learned from Obi-Wan.

Imagine the scene for Luke without this turn toward the mystical force. Imagine that he simply monitors the targeting computer until it says, "Shoot!" When the Death Star explodes, would the scene be as emotionally rich? Most people I ask say that it isn't even close.

Your new tools don't have to be mystical. Any time you learn to put away an old strategy, mindset, or assumptions and use something totally different, you can frame this move as picking up new tools. First, of course, you must think of a time where you had to abandon an earlier way of thinking. Many leaders don't recognize this point or don't want to share it.

The black moment is the moment when the real message of
transformation is going to come. At the darkest moment
comes the light.

— Joseph Campbell[16]

RESURRECTION

This is by far the most advanced story idea I'll share in this book. I'm
even hesitant to include it because I'm afraid students will try to use
it before practicing simpler principles. Trying to use *resurrection*
without developing simple ideas first is likely to make your story a
confusing mess.

The resurrection is a very powerful story arc for a hero to travel.
Many Hollywood films, including most of the animated Pixar
films, incorporate a kind of resurrection.

A heroine on a resurrection arc is inspired by the inciting
incident to pursue a goal. She faces challenges toward achieving the
goal and learns lessons on the way. But despite her best efforts, late
in the story everything she does fails. Her goal is as distant as ever;
her enemies are too strong. She recognizes that all the methods
and tools she has depended on will not work. We call the moment
when all has failed "the moment of no return." The listeners need to
understand emotionally that the heroine has given up. She may be
ashamed that she ever aspired for the goal. She is deeply regretful
that the "at stake" is lost.

After the heroine understands all is lost, she somehow learns that
she needs new tools or approaches that she has never considered
before. Even more powerfully, she learns that what she strove
to attain is not what will fulfill her true and deeper aspiration:
*what she really wanted was something she had until that moment
remained blind to.* She doesn't simply devalue the original goal—
she understands herself and the world better. This gives her a new
goal. When the new goal is achieved with new tools, it gives her a

satisfaction she could never have gotten with her old goal and old tools.

You may recall a famous Cameron Crowe film about a sports agent, *Jerry Maguire*. The agent spends the film desperately working to build a roster with a high-profile athlete/client. When this goal is seemingly accomplished, instead of celebrating with his client, he flies across the country to interrupt a divorced women's party hosted by his estranged wife. There, showing more vulnerability and humility than he ever showed before (new tools), he tells her, "You complete me." The emotional resonance is so powerful that the line is now famous. It resonates because that trip across the country and the heartfelt line show us that Jerry understands that what he thought he wanted will not satisfy him. He learns that what he really wanted was connection with someone left behind, who believed in him even before his success. He had to use the new tools of honesty, vulnerability, and humility to get that. We understand that he has grown into someone far more mature and capable than the man we met at the beginning of the film.

Another way of understanding a resurrecting character is that we witness a transformation. We see *someone give up who they were in order to become something more powerful.* This is why resurrections are so powerful. Giving up who they are, to be something different, is a profound kind of internal growth. The internal journey is by far the most important part of the journey. Everything else is simply data.

But when there is a character resurrection (of some sort) *without* the internal growth, the emotional resonance will miss too. The story will feel hokey. This is why so many action films are great at the action but fail on a deeper emotional level.

To use resurrection in your personal stories you must share a series of challenges that you faced working toward your overarching goal. You can win some challenges. You can lose some. You can achieve your goal, but it is often better if you do not. Then you need to share how you learned that the original goal was not satisfying. Even better, the original goal turned out to be something you found you didn't want at all. A good example is achieving a professional goal and discovering that it made you angry, stressed, or tired. You didn't want that outcome.

You next have to share with your listeners what you did when you learned your goal was not satisfying. Your actions will lead you to take up new tools or new ways of being. This lesson will lead you to a different outcome. Make sure you include a bigger idea (how this affects other people), so listeners will know you're not a self-absorbed and self-satisfied jerk.

When a storyteller can share an honest and vulnerable resurrection, it moves listeners to tears. Listeners don't know *why* the story feels powerful, they only know that it does.

Resurrection Structure:

- The hero is inspired to pursue a goal by an inciting incident.

- The hero faces challenge(s) to achieve the goal and learns lessons on the journey.

- *The point of no return:* The hero reaches a point where she sees that all her efforts will or have failed. All appears lost.

- *Resurrection:* The character abandons her old tools and adopts new tool(s). She changes due to her internal growth. New tools can be a new mind set, strategy, or value.

- The hero learns that what she originally wanted (her goal) would never fulfill her (it is not what she really wanted).

- The hero achieves what she had not understood that she always really wanted. This new thing (a relationship, peace, service) gives her fulfillment.

Now that you see the structure laid out, you probably see how very many of your favorite stories use this structure. It is so common in

Hollywood cinema that, knowing this trope, you may now be able to predict what scenes are coming up next in many films.

This structure is often used in standard sports films, where the hero's goal is to win a particular competition. At some point late in the second act, it looks like she will fail, but in a decisive moment, she will see that her community of friends and family make the difference for her. She learns to value and depend on the team that she had undervalued before. When the story ends, she has learned that what really fulfills her, and the thing she always really wanted, was a community of friends who support one another no matter the score. This is how she *truly* wins. Fadeout. Roll credits.

Make sure any resurrection story you share about yourself is real. If it isn't, you will create a superficial and slimy mess. You can fool some people some of the time, but those of us who see right through you will never trust you again. This of course means that you first have to recognize when you gave something up and learned that you really didn't want what you thought you wanted. This can be the hardest part of sharing a resurrection personal story.

APPENDIX C: EXAMPLE STORIES

Over the years I've heard many amazing stories. I wish I could include them all here. I'm including a few stories that I hope will help you understand how to use the elements and structures I've discussed. Each story is based on a real story shared by someone I know. While I've changed details and names to provide some anonymity, each storyline is true as they remembered it. I didn't choose these stories because they are the best. I chose them for you to see how we used elements to make good stories with real experiences. Each storyteller is a leader in her or his own way.

I crafted the presentation here using the seven elements and structural tools with which you are now familiar. You can see how each element plays its role in making these stories work. Because these are instructional tools, I've included more detail and shared some elements more explicitly than I would in a tight story for a presentation or sharing at a party.

As you read the stories, annotate them: What is the bigger idea? What is the lesson? What contributes to character or setting? You may see ways to make them better. That would be fantastic!

I hope you see that the elements and structures I've shared with you are not a formula. They are tools like musical notes, letting you build an infinite number of stories that relate who you are, what you do, and why your work is important.

STORY BREAKDOWN TEMPLATE

You can use this story breakdown template to help you understand how the seven elements are used in each story. You can fill it out while you read or afterward. It is only a tool to help you learn and notice how the story works. You may think of a better way to tell the story, even shrink it down for a short-time opportunity. If you do, then our plan is working.

Story Intention:

_____

_____

ELEMENTS

Setting
Time: _____

_____

Place: _____

_____

Characters:

_____

Inciting Incident:

Thing Happens:

_____

Thought:

_____

Feeling:

_____

_____

Choice toward a New Goal:

_____

_____

Challenge:

_____

_____

At Stake:

_____

_____

Lessons:

_____

_____

Bigger Idea:

_____

_____

SINGLE-SCENE EXAMPLE STORIES

ISTANBUL SHOPPING – *PHILIP ARMAND*

This is a story Philip shares with filmmakers and people who ask about filmmaking. I hope you feel more connected to him when you learn in part how he has matured in his craft.

Six years ago,
I had been shooting a film in the Middle East for two weeks.
It was about the history of people bombed since the last generation.
We'd already shot in Japan, England, and France.
The director, Josh, and I were finishing up in Istanbul, Turkey
and still recovering from dysentery.
Our cortisol and adrenalin levels were just coming down
because we were so stressed from shooting in Iraq during the war.
It was the first time in two weeks that we had had a rest day.

We were sightseeing,
wandering through the city.
That afternoon we stumbled on a small gift shop
on a quiet side street.
Some of the merchandise was staged on the sidewalk.
As we approached
Josh heard two tourists speaking Mandarin Chinese as they browsed.
Josh proceeded to have a friendly conversation with them
in his nearly perfect Mandarin.
Now,
Joshua is a six-foot-tall Jewish man
who lives in Hoboken, NJ.
He doesn't look like someone who could chat in Mandarin.
The Turkish shopkeeper was leaning in the doorway
and looked really amused.
I was on a small mission to buy a friend Turkish salt and pepper shakers.

So I asked the smiling shopkeeper,
in English,
"Do you speak English?"
He said, "No," and shook his head.
So I asked in German, "Sprechen Sie Deutsch?"
(Do you speak German?)
He said, "Ein bischen." (A little.)
I could tell we couldn't communicate very much.
The Chinese people left
and some French tourists wandered over.
Josh started to converse with them in French.
The shopkeeper noticed Josh's new conversation.
I realized in this moment
that it was in fact really unusual to see American tourists
so language-ready.
I knew that between Josh and me, we were conversant in six
languages.
I speak German, Romanian, and English.
Josh speaks French, Mandarin, Arabic, German,
and of course, English.
I wandered past the storekeeper and into the store.
He followed me as I browsed,
and I noticed he was nodding his head
as if he knew something special.
In a few minutes he said,
"Ah ha!"
Loudly.
He used a tone that indicated that
he just discovered something.
I was the only person in the store.
I turned to him
and raised my eyebrows
because I was confused.
He pointed directly at me
and said,
"CIA.

Ah ha!"
And he looked back and forth between me and Josh outside.
I said,
"No. No! NO!
 No CIA!
We are filmmakers.
Journalists!"
He said,
"Sure!
Many people who make movies speak many languages."
He winked at me to let me know
that we shared a special secret together.
He formed his hand into a gun shape
and shot silent secret bullets at me in a playful way.

I felt uncomfortable.
I knew that as Josh and I traveled through warring countries,
in areas getting bombed by Americans,
it is mortally important that we weren't confused with secret
government agencies.
In this moment,
I didn't know how to convince this storekeeper
that I wasn't a spy.
That I wasn't a political operative.
All I could do was wander away from him.
He continued shooting make-believe bullets at me.
I bought some ceramic thimbles and left
as quickly as I could.

Epilogue
I think telling the true stories
of people around the world is really important.
Important enough to risk danger to tell them.
I think it humanizes foreign strangers
and actually saves lives.
Especially in times of war.

Of all the places I've been,
This experience stays with me.
It made me reconsider my own preconceived ideas.
I got that this storekeeper thinks he met CIA agents
simply because he met Americans proficient in languages other
than English.
I wonder,
as I've traveled around the world
documenting stories,
how much I got wrong
because my assumptions were as strong as the shopkeeper's.

I learned
that I need to be more aware
about how my actions are interpreted.
I understand even more
how my own traveling,
with camera gear,
as a white man in violent places
is unusual.

And people make unusual assumptions about me.
I realize now that I may have put myself in more danger
than I ever thought.
Even worse,
I have likely put my companions,
crew,
and local helpers
into more danger than I ever considered.
I'm not sure how to avoid being confused with the CIA.
I am more aware,
that I need to consider that new friends
may assume I'm doing research on how to bomb them.
It is always a possibility
and that colors my conversations.

Philip Story Breakdown

Story Intention:

Share how I've grown to be a more responsible international filmmaker and care for my crew far better than inexperienced filmmakers. Create humor (when the storekeeper shouts "CIA"), and empathy when sharing insight about unwittingly putting crew and helpers in danger.

ELEMENTS

Setting:

Time: Afternoon on a rest day, six years ago, during the American war in Iraq after two weeks' constant shooting.

Place: Istanbul sidewalk gift shop.

Characters:

- Director Josh
- Shopkeeper

Inciting Incident:

Thing Happens: He pointed directly at me and said, "CIA. Ah Ha!"

Thought: "You misunderstand. This could be dangerous." (*implied*)

Feeling: Surprise, concern. (*implied*)

New Goal: Get properly identified as a filmmaker/journalist in the store and the future. (*goal is never achieved*)

Choice toward a New Goal: I'm going to protect my crew more in the future.

Challenge:

- Getting identified accurately as a journalist.

At Stake:

The safety of me, my crew, local helpers. (*Bigger*) Saving lives by telling stories about strange foreigners to support peace and understanding.

Lessons:

- My own assumptions may be as misleading as those of the shopkeeper.

- I may have put myself and crew in more danger than I understood.

- I need to take more actions to identify myself as a journalist whenever I'm in a dangerous place where Americans can be a threat.

Bigger Idea:

I will keep my crew and local helpers safer because I learned from this experience. I'll continue to tell stories that foster peace.

I'LL BE THAT WAY, TOO — *LOIS WONG*

Single Scene
My father died in December 1962.
I was seven years old,
living on Stockton Street,
right in San Francisco's Chinatown.
It was a difficult time.
My mother became a single parent.
We had to find another income.
Our whole lives hurt.

I remember one afternoon
in the first week of January,
Mr. Dennis Chong visited my mother
in our apartment living room.
He and his wife had visited several times
in the weeks since my Dad died.
That day he gave her some money.
I remember my mother crying.

When he walked out our door,
my mother turned to me,
tears on her face,
and she said,
"He is the only person who helped us."

I was so scared at that time.
I didn't know how we would survive
and I thought,
"I am going to be like him
when I grow up."

Epilogue
It is no accident that I'm now Board Chair
for Chinese American Children's Services.

The difference Dennis Chong made to my family
in our most difficult time
still fills my heart.
In many ways,
all I'm doing
is inviting other people
to be a kind of Dennis Chong
in our own ways.
I promise you,
we make a difference.
I've known since 1962.

Lois Story Breakdown

Story Intention:
Share what inspires me to work for Chinese American Children's Services.

ELEMENTS

Setting:
Time: One afternoon in the first week of January 1963.
Place: My family apartment on Stockton Street in San Francisco's Chinatown.

Characters:

- Mother
- Mr. Dennis Chong

Inciting Incident:
Thing Happens: She said, "He is the only one who helped us."
Thought: I want to be like him when I grow up.
Feeling: Afraid, thankful (*implied*)
Choice toward a New Goal: Grow up to be as attentive and generous as Dennis Chong.

Challenge:

- Family is recovering from my father's death.
- Few people have helped us.

At Stake:

- My family's well-being.

Lessons:

- People who offer to help can make a huge difference when help is needed most.

- I want to be someone who makes a difference when others are in trouble.

Bigger Idea:

- I have committed much of my life to helping children who need stability and support growing up in difficult situations.

MULTISCENE STORY EXAMPLES

SUCCESS IS NOT A POPULARITY GAME – *JAMES CHANG*

Scene 1: The Shock

I remember specifically it was June 10, 2010, at 4 p.m.
I was in the meeting room in a high-rise building,
at Queens Asset Management,
a hedge fund in Shanghai.
I was a junior analyst
and I had been at the firm only three months.
I knew I was good enough to earn a spot there
but I also knew that
compared to the others
I knew almost nothing.

Rita was one of just three portfolio managers
and she was a rebel.
Her investment style was nothing like the others'.
I remember that June day
because that's when Rita
approached me
to explain that we would work together.
She told me to look only for
poorly performing companies.
Those were the only kind she invested in.
I was shocked and amazed.

I had been studying finance for a year at that time.
In everything I learned,
good investors look for good companies.
And that seemed
obvious.
Who wants losers?
So you can imagine how surprising it was
when Rita said the opposite.

I wondered what she could possibly know.
To me, it sounded either genius
or totally stupid.

That was the first conversation I ever had with someone
who was a "value investor."

She explained to me
that if together
we could find a single company
that looked bad to everyone else,
it could give us far better returns than conventional strategies
If
we could find something others didn't see.

We would search for a single company
not yet showing the world
what they could do.
When we found one,
my job would be to wait
patiently,
Trusting that my research was valid
to get our kind of success.
I didn't know then that the waiting and trusting
would be the hardest part.

While finding poor performers was an exciting idea,
it was not
the most exciting part of the work.
What was more exciting,
was how investing this way
did something that the other strategies
just didn't do.

Value investing actually helps companies
that could be great

and are in difficult times.
More specifically,
the strategy helps people trying to build great companies
who are ignored by everyone else.
That was way more exciting
than anything I had read in my textbooks.

Starting with Rita,
I felt inspired.
I was so happy to work with someone
who was actually using capital to support people,
creating new jobs
and growing the economy.

Scene 2: The Journey Begins
That night
I bought books about distressed value investing.
I stayed up late at home over the next month
reading as many books on this as I could.
I discovered investment masters who used this strategy
like John Templeton,
Peter Lynch,
and Marty Whitman.

The whole strategy made sense to me
because we were finding value
in places others ignored.

So all of my work went into finding bad-looking companies.
But there was a problem.

Scene 3: The Rejection
Every day when I returned to the office
over the next month,
I was still just a junior analyst,

and my job was to make investment recommendations.
and I was the only junior analyst recommending companies
that looked like dogs.

In an industry where success comes from impressing colleagues,
it was dangerous to recommend companies
that my colleagues
and the market
all agreed were terrible.

Of course that's why I picked them!
They were terrible at the time.

I remember sitting in our corporate dining room
and all three of my junior analyst colleagues,
Wen, Ming, and Mark,
ignored me at lunch.
They wouldn't sit near me.
They didn't want to be seen talking with me.
They didn't want to be associated with the loser-picker.

Scene 4: The Wisdom
The first week of August that year,
I had researched distressed companies for two months,
When Rita gave me the wisdom I needed to hear
as my colleagues distanced themselves from me.
"Investments are never good
because people agree with us,
they're good because they work."
She was asking me to be braver
than my colleagues.
She was asking me to learn what they could not see.

She offered me a test
that was also a vote of confidence.
She would invest $20 million

solely
on my recommendations.

I would have twelve months
to show that I could produce better returns than my peers.
Obviously, if I lost $20 million
I would lose my job,
whatever credibility I might have had,
and would probably have wasted the whole year.

So on my recommendation
Rita put $20 million in a Chinese hotel chain
because I thought the company would merge with a competitor
and I thought the value would jump at least 50 percent.

Scene 5: Rocky Times
Eight weeks later
I saw from our tracking software
That the stock had gone
down
15 percent!
She
(and I)
lost $3 million.
in eight weeks!

That was more money than my family had earned
in three generations.
I still feel deep respect for
how much Rita trusted me.
She gave me the trust
and experience
I needed to grow emotionally strong
for this field.

Fortunately

Wen, Ming, and Mark didn't know how much I'd lost
with my first loser company.

Scene 6: Success Revealed
In the second week of November
I was home at 10 p.m.
when I was sitting at my computer
and saw
that our poor-performing hotel group
had made the merger!

I saw Rita hours later
when we both were in the office.
I was so thrilled,
but she was not nearly as surprised as I was.
She reminded me
that she always thought that I was right
and
that's why she put the money down.

It was an extremely exciting day for me.
It still is.
For Rita
it was just another day in the market.

After ninety days
we got our 50 percent return!
That meant a $10 million gain
in three months!
None of the other junior analysts did that.

Epilogue
I'm sharing this story
Because I learned
huge lessons
working with Rita.

By far the biggest
is that to make extraordinary results
I have to research
until I see what others miss
And then
I have to be brave enough
to act on it.
This means brave enough
to go against the crowd.

I also learned that my investing success
has nothing to do
with whether the big market thinks my ideas are good.
My success is about
the return my team creates
Because we do good work.

I also learned the importance of picking the right team members.
I need members willing to take risks
when they think the work is solid
and trust the work,
not rumors
or less-informed opinions.

Lastly,
I share this story because this is how I learned
there is a way for me to use my education,
my skills,
and resources
to invest in Chinese people
who are not *yet* great
but will be.

I know I can be one of the investors
in a small minority
who are willing to invest

in the future,
as opposed to past success.
I think this is important for any country.
And this is the only way to find the future
"rocket ship" companies.
I'm going to be a builder for the future,
not simply a follower of the past.

If the lessons Rita taught me are right,
I can I give returns to my clients,
and invest in the future of China
now that China is ready for it.

James Story Breakdown

Story Intention:

Share what I've learned, what I do, and why it matters. Inspire connection and inspiration.

ELEMENTS:

Setting:

Time: June 10, 2010, at 4 p.m., three months after starting at the firm.

Place: High-rise meeting room at Queens Asset Management hedge fund in Shanghai.

Characters:

- Rita, the portfolio manager.
- Junior analyst colleagues Wen, Ming, and Mark.

Inciting Incident:

Thing Happens: She told me to find only poorly performing companies.

Thought: This is against everything I've learned. You know, something genius or stupid. (*implied*)

Feeling: Shocked and amazed.

Choice toward a New Goal: Learn if this is genius or stupid; outperform others with a rebel method.

Challenge:

Colleagues shun me. I can't maintain respect in the company because I suggest bad companies that no one else in the company or market considers good.

At Stake:

$20 million, my career aspirations. (*bigger*) The success of corporate leaders building future great companies in China, but which the market doesn't yet believe in.

Lessons:

- My investing success has nothing to do with whether the big market thinks my ideas are good.

- My success is about the return my team creates because we do good work.

- I have to research until I see what others miss.

- Be brave enough to act on my research and go against the crowd.

- I must pick a team willing to take risks when they trust the work.

- My team must trust their work, not the rumors or less-informed opinions.

Bigger Idea:

My clients will get results far beyond those of less brave and informed investors. China will grow faster and stronger because investors like me support the people creating great companies instead of betting on past success.

MALARIA IN THE BUSH—*VICTOR MUTAI*

Scene 1: Danger Descends
    In June 2005 the rain had come
    To my boarding high school, Nakuru, in Kenya.
    With the rain came the mosquitoes,
    And that year,
    A terrible wave of malaria.

    For those who don't know,
    malaria is caused by a parasite
    that's transmitted by mosquitoes.
    The parasite breeds inside our joints.
    This means for someone with malaria
    literally their whole body hurts
    as the parasite multiplies inside.
    Well over 1 million people die from malaria each year.
    Most of them are in Africa.

    Since I was the head prefect of the school,
    I made rounds to check on students.
    I saw over 100 sick students
    and saw many of them couldn't even leave to get food.
    Even as a native Kenyan,
    I became worried.
    I knew they weren't getting appropriate care.

    In our school of 1,600 students plus faculty
    there was only one nurse.
    All she could do was give an over-the-counter painkiller.
    This does not kill the parasites
    or heal bodies.

Scene 2: The Journey Begins
    On Monday,
    in my unique capacity as head prefect,

I went to Principal Kirui in his office
and told him we needed a doctor right away.
He was uninterested.
Maybe he was worried about the expense.
Maybe he thought we were overdramatic.

Scene 3: Persistence
I returned to him on Wednesday
and told him again.
Again, he turned me away.
I don't think he knew how bad it was.

Scene 4: More Persistence
When I went back on Friday,
he told me he was tired of hearing from me!
This was not the time
for me to be concerned about myself!

Scene 5: A Plan Is Made
That evening I gathered over thirty of my prefects
in the big dining hall.
We agreed to take all of our sick students
to the nurse
that very evening.

Scene 6: The Call Goes Out
After all the students reached the office,
I got on the school radio
and announced to all administrators
and faculty
that we had a problem!
Over 100 students were lined up waiting for care.
Some were extremely sick.
When the administration and security officers showed up,
they saw the hall filled with sick students.

Administrator Ngeno arrived first
and was so surprised
she asked me why I hadn't reported this earlier!
She and the principal got on the radio
to call in all the resident teachers
and all the other security officers
and then,
for the first time in the school's history,
I watched them call the hospital for help.
Several doctors came.

It took hours that night for every student to be treated.
I stayed up all night helping get out medicine,
Coordinating,
and monitoring students.

That night five were sent to the hospital
because they needed serious care.
I wonder what would have happened
if we hadn't gotten more help.

Epilogue

I learned that waiting for authority to take action
may not serve people we care about.

I learned it is important for authority to see a problem directly.
Big problems can be hard to see
if they are presented piecemeal.

I also learned that, by organizing people together,
problems can be addressed in ways that seemed impossible moments
earlier.
I'm still proud of getting those students medical care.
They all survived.
And I grew up a lot.

Victor Malaria Story Breakdown

Story Intention:
Share my formation as a leader who will confront authority and organize peers to get help where it is needed. Inspire courage, collaboration, and persistence.

ELEMENTS:

Setting:
Time: June 2005 while I served as Head Prefect.
Place: Nakuru Boarding High School in Kenya.

Characters:

- Over 100 sick students
- Principle Kirui
- Thirty prefects
- Administrator Mrs. Ngeno

Inciting Incident:
Thing Happens: Saw over 100 sick students in their dorms.
Thought: They could die and need more help.
Feeling: Worried, committed. (*implied*)
Choice toward a New Goal: Save the lives of my classmates.

Challenge:

- School does not have enough resources.
- We don't have access to a doctor.
- Principle Kirui won't call for a doctor.

At Stake:

- The health and lives of classmates.

- The health and lives of classmates similarly endangered in the future.

Lessons:

- I learned it is important for authority to see a problem directly.
- Be a leader even when authority dismisses me.
- Big problems can be hard to see if they are presented piecemeal.
- By organizing people together, problems can be addressed in ways that seemed impossible moments earlier.

Bigger Idea:

- Sick students got medical help.
- Some students may have had their lives saved.
- Future students may get medical attention when they are critically ill.
- I will make a difference for others when they are in need because I learned how to inspire action by authority in a new way.

THE NEW PREFECT—*VICTOR MUTAI*

Scene 1: The Thirst Begins
>In approximately 1987
>in the height of the rainy season
>I was born in Chemaetany Village,
>a rural place in the Rift Valley Province of Kenya.
>No one in my family knows exactly when I was born.
>
>
>In 1995 I was in the third grade
>when I read an illustrated book titled
>*A Journey to the Moon.*
>After that,
>I was inspired
>And wanted to be an astronaut to go to the moon.
>I didn't even really know what that meant yet.
>It was an illustrated book
>And I didn't even speak English.
>But I wanted to go to space.
>So I went to the library
>And found a book on the astronaut Neil Armstrong
>And another on combustion.
>This had to do with chemistry and energy.
>Somehow I knew this was important for being an astronaut.
>I thirsted for a life beyond our village
>And the education that could get me there.

Scene 2: Support an Orphan
>Unfortunately,
>my parents died when I was in the fourth grade.
>I had six sisters
>and one brother.
>All my sisters had to drop out of school
>because we couldn't afford their tuition.
>I was among the best students in my class.
>I remember my teacher, Mr. Kenbakor,

told me in his tiny office
next to my abandoned kindergarten classroom
that he would keep me in the class
even though we couldn't afford the tuition of $5 a year.
He knew I had no parents to pay it.
He knew my family depended on me.
He gave me his own type of scholarship.
I call it a free pass.

Scene 3: Surviving

But we needed money to buy necessities like food and clothing.
We resorted to making charcoal in the Chepalungu Forest illegally.
The rangers would arrest us if they caught us.
This meant we had to go deep into the forest and haul out the charcoal in the middle of the night.
I remember when I was in seventh grade,
I was scared
and hauling six sacks out of the forest on donkeys.
It was after midnight,
raining and dark.
I had stop and sit down to pull thorns out of my feet.
We couldn't afford shoes so the vegetation would cut up and stick in our feet.
There is nothing worse than a thorn in your foot in the jungle rain.
Sometimes it would become infected and I'd have to limp for a week.
This is all we knew to do to survive.
I learned to do whatever it takes to survive.
My sisters would continue to do this for five years.

Scene 4: To Boarding School

I graduated at the top of my division in Grade 8.
Out of thirty-two students
only three of us went to high school that year.

Unfortunately, this meant
only three of us had a promise of a better life.
Without education
we were all stuck in a rural village
without water,
electricity,
or healthcare.

My sisters sold four
of our seven cows
to pay for the first year of my boarding high school.
In fact,
when we got to my school
we had so little money
that my sister Jane couldn't even return home.
She was stuck in my school town for a week
waiting for the family to send money for her return.

Scene 5: Danger Awaits

When I got to Nakuru High School
I was one of 400 students in my class.
I was happy to get to build a better life for me and my siblings.
They were all depending on me
and supporting me.

Unfortunately,
when I arrived for my first day in February,
that night,
all the older students came to the freshmen,
picked through our bags,
and took everything of any value.
This included food
and money.
I didn't have money to steal
and only one uniform, which I was wearing.

I also learned Nakuru was a dangerous place.
The seniors bullied the freshmen.
They even forced us to do their washing,
stole our food,
and they beat me up.
I had to wake at 4 a.m. most mornings
to wash their clothes.

Scene 6: Violence Present

I remember the worst bully that year was
Tony Rivera.
He was big
and his father was the head principal.
So the school wouldn't discipline him.

He beat a freshman in my class at the reservoir
where we all had to wash our clothes.
I knew that I had to go to the reservoir every day
to wash my only set of clothes.

Scene 7: Danger United

One Saturday night
more than ten school prefects,
who are student administrators,
called 100 freshmen into
our dorm, Nakuru House.
There they beat all of us for an hour
with bars of soap
swung in a towel.

I understood that the school prefects
would protect all the seniors.
If any underclassmen reported a senior,
then all the seniors and prefects
would mistreat us.
This included beating us in our rooms.

Tony and others beat as many students as they wanted to
and were never punished.
Not only could we not defend ourselves,
we had no justice system to turn to.

I was beaten by upperclassmen at least five times that year.

Scene 8: Discovered a Scholarship

I knew my siblings could not afford my tuition
for the following year.
They spent over half the family wealth
just to pay for the first year.

That year,
at a morning assembly
I heard that principal Kendakor created a scholarship program.
Where students would be credited 2000 Kenya shillings
for every full course A.
That was about $30.
2000 shillings could buy a uniform, shoes, and writing books all
together.
My sister took over a week to get 100 shillings.
I figured out that if I took extra classes
and I got A's in every class
that I could earn enough scholarship funds to pay for the whole
tuition for each coming year.
You see, getting an A in only the required classes wouldn't be
enough.

This meant I had to take twelve classes—
30 percent more than the requirements.
But for me this was the minimum
so I could return.
All I had to do was get an A
in everything
all the time.

I was in the biggest school in the country.
There were 400 students in my class alone.
And 1,600 in the school.
I just had to be better than everybody else.
When I heard about the scholarship,
I committed right then.

If I could,
I would use my final year's winnings
to pay for my brother's tuition
when he arrived my senior year.

It was even harder than I thought it would be.
The only way to get an A
was to get an A
on about every single test
in every class
every semester.

Scene 9—Help for Applications
It worked!
But there was a problem.
In January of my Junior year
we didn't have money for me to bus back to school on time from
break.
This meant I was late by a week
And missed twelve exams.
I dropped from the best student
To number 157.

Principal Kendakor noticed the problem,
brought me into his office
and helped me apply for a different scholarship.
When I got it,
I earned myself back to the number one position.

But I learned how absolutely precarious this challenge was
and I never went home for a break again.

Scene 10: New Head Prefect
    The next year would be my senior year.
    In November,
    the last month of the academic year,
    an assembly was called to select the next prefects.
    I had withheld my name from nominations
    because I was focused on academics.
    When the vote came,
    I was surprised and happy
    when hundreds of students began
    chanting my name.
    A few minutes later
    the new principal,
    Mr. Kirui,
    announced I was the new
    head prefect
    for the whole school.
    I felt both scared and excited.
    I took the responsibility very seriously.
    I knew I had so much power,
    they would even let me beat
    all the students I wanted to.
    And
    I remembered all the fear
    And pain
    I experienced
    just trying to make a better life for my family
    and decided that day
    that the abuse culture at Nakuru
    would end.

Scene 11: The Milk Standoff

You must understand
that the school was severely under resourced.
Among many things,
there was not enough food.
This meant that students would line up as early as possible
to get some food.
But because of the bullying,
and seniority abuse,
the seniors would cut in line,
steal food
and underclassmen would go to class
or bed
with nothing.
Even worse,
seniors assigned VIP privileges to their own family and friends
who were not even seniors.
This meant hundreds of students
didn't get food
no matter how much they played by the rules.

Having come from a poor rural village
from a family who couldn't even afford our own shoes,
I was tired of watching bullies steal from new students.

I started by example.
I stood in the food line myself
and never stole food.
I made my brother do the same.
On seeing this,
All 400 seniors were shamed to end their own food stealing.

I remember one specific Saturday evening in January 2005.
I was eighteen years old,
and the head prefect
for the year that had just begun.

The school offered milk only twice a week.
And for the three years as an underclassman
I almost never got milk,
Because the seniors cut in line,
with big containers,
and took all of it.
On my first week as head prefect
I decided this would end.
So,
I served the milk myself!
I gave everyone
a single cup.

Now,
Tony had graduated earlier.
Jitu was the new biggest bully of over 700 boys at the time.
He came from a gang-ridden town,
and he was over six foot tall,
which is tall in an undernourished Kenya.
He even told others that he'd killed someone,
and because of his hometown
we believed him.

On that first milk serving
Jitu came to the front of the line
held up a five-liter container
and told me to fill it up.
I gave him a single cup.

I don't remember exactly what he said to me next.
I do remember he was much taller.
And he grabbed my shirt.
And then physically pulled me over the top of the serving table
to his side.
Holding my shirt with both of his hands
he demanded to take as much as he wanted.

I understood his anger
because I knew he watched seniors
for three years
do the same thing.
He wanted his turn.
I'm still surprised today
that I wasn't afraid.
It may have been because I'd been bullied so long
by so many bullies
when I just wanted to get an education
that maybe I got used to it.
What I did know
was that I was now taking a stand.
I was doing something I had never done before
And I would bear whatever the cost.

I don't remember how this conversation ended.
I do remember
that for the first time in the school's history
other prefects
ran to me
and separated us
so I *wouldn't* get hurt.

I also remember the room was filled
with more than 400 people.
And they watched
for the first time
seniors denied stealing from underclassmen.

That was the beginning of a new campaign
so all students could be safe at school.

In my memory
that was the turning point.
When the 400 seniors saw I was serious,

saw my stand,
and reflected on their own experience,
they joined me.

I felt shocked and inspired.
I learned that others wanted a safe
and fair culture,
they just didn't know how to create it.

Scene 12: The Surprise Ending
In November 2005
it was near the end of my year as head prefect.
As per protocol,
I was silently studying in classroom 4W along with fifty-nine
classmates that evening.
Jitu came in all the way from his own class, 4F,
across campus.
He was of course the bully who pulled me across the milk table in
January.
Everyone knew it.

He stood in the front of our class of sixty
and did something that I couldn't envision
and still moves me today.
He apologized for that first week
when he bullied me for milk.
He thought at the time I was withholding milk
to demonstrate my new power.
He saw later that I was doing it on principle.
And when he got that,
he knew he was wrong.

He wanted that not only I know this
but our whole class know it before we graduated.

I was deeply moved.

I'm deeply moved now remembering it.
In fact, I really wish I could have recorded that moment.

When Jitu made that apology
That moment taught me that I had made a difference.

It taught me that it took time
but my principles
by my example
had been communicated.
It also taught me that when they were communicated
even to the most feared bully at my school,
he could change.
It inspired me to think what more I could change
by standing in principle.

Epilogue

I've learned a lot from the journey
as an orphan in a small village
to the Gothic halls of Yale.

I promise you
there were times I was afraid for my life.
And because of my poor family,
afraid for their welfare if I got hurt.

One of the most important lessons I got
was that I am surprised at who will help me.
People help me even if they never say they would.

I learned that while it's both difficult,
and dangerous,
it's possible to curb a tradition of oppression.
It can take a single person to acknowledge tyranny
for change to begin.

I learned even in a place with a tradition of oppression,
if I speak out based on my principles
and practice consistent with them,
other people notice.

I also learned it can inspire them in ways I didn't know I could.
In short, I learned the difference one person can make
standing on principle in the face of danger.

I'm so thankful I can be here now
sharing this story with you.

Victor Prefect Story Breakdown

Story Intention:

Share how I've grown as a leader and how deep my passion for justice goes. Share inspiration and hope.

ELEMENTS:

Setting:

Time: 1985, in the third grade through high school
Place: Rural Kenya.

Characters:

- Six sisters
- Sister Jane
- Mr. Kenbakor
- Tony Rivera
- School prefects
- Principle Mr. Kirui
- Jitu the bully

Inciting Incident:

Thing Happens: Read *A Journey to Space*.
Thought: I want to go to space.
Feeling: inspired, excited (*implied*)
New Goal: Become an astronaut and get an education that will allow me to do this.

Challenge:

- Can't afford tuition.

- Must take extra classes and get an A in every class.

- Bullies beat me.

- Bullies force me to do their work.

- Bullies steal my food.

At Stake:

- My dream.

- A better life.

- The welfare of my family.

- My safety.

- (*Bigger*) Justice and peace.

Lessons:

- If I stood up to bullies I might be surprised at who would help me.

- People will help me even if they haven't yet indicated they would.

- It's possible to curb a tradition of oppression.

- It can take just one person to acknowledge tyranny for change to begin.

- I can inspire others in ways I didn't understand before.

- I learned the difference one person can make simply standing on principle in the face of danger.

Bigger Idea:

- The current and future students at the school would be safer and experience a culture of justice more than ever before.

- The bullies changed, and future students would not be abused.

- I will use these lessons to create justice and peace in the future, in ways I didn't know I could before.

MY KIND OF SUCCESS — *ALASTAIR ONG*

Alastair's story is included because it's a classic entrepreneur origin story and it's real. Notice how he clearly includes a bigger idea from the beginning and that he learns a big lesson that points to an even bigger big idea at the end.

Scene 1: Surprise News
> In the summer of 2005
> I was at my mother's home on Long Island.
> My parents are Chinese Filipinos.
> My mother told me that she gave money to my aunt
> to give to my cousin
> who would fly it to the Philippines.
> I asked why she didn't just use Western Union to send the money.
> She explained that they charged 25 percent.
> In other words, for a $5 transfer,
> the cost was 200 pesos.
> 200 pesos would buy food for a day!

Scene 2: This Is Big
> That week I read an article in the *Wall Street Journal*
> that explained that Filipinos were flying
> bundles of money on planes
> to get remittances home
> because of the exorbitant transfer fees.
> 80 percent of the country's GDP
> was dependent on remittances from abroad.
>
> That's how I learned that my mother
> was one of millions of Filipinos
> transporting money back on planes.
>
> I was excited.
> I thought,
> I could build a company that could make money on this.

Scene 3: The Pitch

> Weeks later I was in the Manila Hotel.
> It is a holdover from the colonial times
> and still the nicest hotel in the country.
> In one of their private dining rooms
> I met with three investors and pitched an investment fund.
> At one point, I mentioned by surprise my idea for a remittance company
> and I could see their eyes get wide.
> When they blinked,
> I could see dollar signs in their eyes.
> I knew they were really excited.
> It was time to pitch *that* company.

Scene 4: We're On

> A week later,
> about noon,
> I was in my cousin's house in central Manila
> playing with his aquarium and fish
> when I got a call from a money manager named Brenda.
> She told me that one of my pitches had gone really well.
> My first investor was Luisa Estrada,
> a current senator and former first lady in the Philippines.
> She was someone with enormous power in the country.
> She was ready to put half a million up front right away.
> I was ecstatic.
> I wouldn't have to fund-raise any longer!
> But the joy didn't last long
> Because there was a lot of work to do.

Scene 5: The Journey Is On

> That month I opened an office in Manila
> and hired a ten-person programming team.
> I learned everything takes three times longer than I expected.
> The programming took a year.
> I was still so excited to start making this work!

Scene 6: Stuck
> Because of Luisa's importance,
> I met with the CEOs of the country's top six banks.
> Each told us they were really excited about working with us.
> But after six months
> we still couldn't get a deal done.
> I remember sitting in a meeting with a CEO in his high office
> with his managers
> and hearing him tell his managers
> with his own mouth
> to get the deal done
> and get us the tech specifics we needed.
> But when I left the meeting
> I never heard from any of the staff again.
> It was like I was never there.
>
> I now understand that the managers
> didn't have their own technology ready,
> And they didn't want to fail.
> Nor did they think
> they'd get credit for any success.
> So they didn't really want to follow up.

Scene 7: Crack of Light
> For a whole year I failed to find a banking partner,
> even with a nationally powerful investor.
> I went to brunch with my cousin Ivan
> and his best friend Johnathan
> at the Wack-Wack Golf Club,
> the only golf club in Manila.
> We sat outside on the patio deck.
> Johnathan mentioned that he worked at Security Bank,
> which was the seventh largest bank in the Philippines.
>
> The banking system in the Philippines, he explained,
> was like US banking in the 1960s.

It was still very difficult to transfer funds from one bank to another.
He told me that he worked in "conjurnetics."
I had no idea what that meant.
It turned out he worked on generating new business.
I asked for more,
and he explained they had a pay system
where employers could pay simply by transferring money to a Visa debit card.
This was super advanced in the Philippines.

I was elated.
I knew right away that *this*
was the system we were looking for.
Right at brunch, we set up a meeting to follow up with Security Bank.

Scene 8: Welcome Arms
Five days later I walked into the Security Bank headquarters
just two miles from our office.
It was about twenty stories tall.
When I walked into their biggest conference room
on their top floor
I felt great.
When I saw they had gathered ten people to meet us
and served a full buffet
with a drinks bar
to welcome us,
I felt accepted.
I learned that day that we had found our banking partner.

They figured out we were going to make them a lot of money.
A week later I returned to the same top-floor conference room.
This time
the press was there to cover our partnership agreement signing.
We made the front page of the *Manila Bulletin*,
the biggest paper in Manila.

I felt confident because I knew
Security Bank saw how big this was going to be.
My team created a platform
that did real-time transfers
that charged only 4 percent
and had a $50 ceiling for the fee!

Scene 9: A New Partner

Six months later I met a guy named Sy in the Manila Hotel.
We sat in the middle of the Open Air Cafe
where he told me that he represented three investors
who wanted to buy our company.
We hadn't even launched yet,
so we didn't even have any sales,
but they could see the potential.

Scene 10: A New Path

Two weeks later Sy showed up at our office with three technical
people.
Their tech team sat with our tech team
and discussed our technical setup.
I sat with Sy and showed him all our legal documents,
incorporation, and contracts.
The due diligence went on for three months.

Sy and his team learned everything about us.
We even sent code to his programmers
and he wrote me how much they liked it.

Scene 11: Success

In November 2007
Sy came to my office with a deal to buy the company.
When I signed the documents in our conference room on the eighth
floor,
the agreement was I would get $4 million
if the company didn't make *any* money,

but up to $10 million if sales went well.
I also built into the deal
that my ten employees couldn't be fired for two years.
We felt great.
My whole team went to a karaoke bar and celebrated
for six hours.

The first payment was $1 million cash.
I became a millionaire with that single deal.

Scene 12: Strange Things

Saturday,
the very next day,
I was at my cousin's house
and I got a notification on my phone that the company server was down.
I was confused.
This was uncommon,
and I knew no one was working on a Saturday.
But this didn't seem like a problem because we had redundancy.
There was nothing to be alarmed about.

Scene 13: More Strange Things

I got the same notification on Sunday.
I was surprised and confused as to why they were still down.
When I got the same notification early Monday morning
I got nervous.
I knew something was wrong.
At 10 a.m. on Monday
I logged onto our servers and discovered that the servers
were *physically* shut down.

This meant that all of our *redundancy* was *also* shut down.
I was *really* confused.
I contacted our main programmer, Bong,
and he told me that Sy had instructed him to take down our entire

site.
Bong didn't know why.
Then Bong told me that when he got to work that day
he and all the other programmers were assigned to work at offices of
Western Union.

I called Sy next
and asked if his investors were
Western Union.
He told me they were subsidiaries of Western Union.

I felt duped
and cheated.
I had built this company for two years,
made banking deals that had never existed in the Philippines before,
and now I learned that Western Union had tricked me into selling it to them
so that they could shut it down.
They also had all our proprietary software,
and I knew they could use it for whatever they wanted,
which could include
exploitive prices.

Scene 14: Retreat

A week later I flew to the Thai island Koh Phi Phi.
I went because the beaches are remote and beautiful,
and there's amazing food nearby.
I sat on a beach watching the surf.
I had a coconut water in my hands
and a baseball cap keeping the sun out of my eyes.

I had nowhere I needed to go
and I could buy whatever I wanted.

And I had this thought:
"I am *not* happier."
It didn't matter that I was a new millionaire on vacation.
It didn't matter that I could do whatever I wanted.
It didn't matter that I could stay as long as I wanted.

That's the moment when I learned that money
doesn't make me happy.
I was still feeling shock.

I could see that I had started the company just for me.
All my motivations were really selfish.
I wanted money to spend on me,
my wife,
my family,
and my friends.
A tiny little community chosen by me.
And I got it.

Epilogue

With the company destroyed,
I could see for the first time
that I *really* cared about millions of Filipinos being exploited
by a banking system incentivized
to take as much from them as it can.
And those Filipinos have no good option.
In fact, that banking system fooled me.

I've checked in with the programmers.
They are still working for Western Union.
And they make double what I paid them at the start-up.
I'm delighted to know this.
I also know that Luisa got her investment back with 20 percent returns.
She is happy.

When I reflected on
not only those two years working with my team
but also the years I spent with other companies,
my family,
and so many friends,
what I learned from those two years is that
people make me happy.
Even more,
helping people makes me happy.

This could be a story about getting duped,
or becoming a successful entrepreneur,
or becoming a millionaire.
And it is.
But what's most important to me
is that it's the story of how I learned to be generous.
And this is how I prioritize my life now.
Because this lesson changed my life more than all the rest combined.

Alastair Story Breakdown

Story Intention:
Share my priorities and my maturation as a business leader, investor, and philanthropist.

ELEMENTS:

Setting:
Time: Summer 2005.
Place: Mother's home on Long Island.

Characters:

- Mother
- Cousin Ivan
- Brenda
- Luisa Estrada (the senator)
- Bank CEO
- Sy
- Bong

Inciting Incident:
Thing Happens: Read that 80 percent of Filipino GDP was dependent on remittances and connect that with Filipinos who are flying it all on planes.
Thought: I could create a company to make money on this.
Feeling: Excited, hopeful (*implied*)
Choice toward a New Goal: Make money making a better option for Filipinos than costly Western Union transfers or flying home.

Challenge:

- Get funding.
- Find a banking partner.

At Stake:

- Personal financial success.
- (*Bigger*) The financial health of millions of Filipinos.

Lessons:

- Conjurnetics has to do with business development.
- Security Bank was willing to collaborate.
- I got duped.
- I was acting selfishly.
- Money doesn't make me happy.
- People make me happy.
- Helping people makes me more happy.

Bigger Idea:
I now use my skills, opportunities, and experiences to find ways to help people instead of how to spend more money on my tiny group of friends and family.

A LAST WORD FROM CHARLES

You got this far and so I'm assuming you found something that made you stronger and more effective. You may never know how much this delights me.

While I wish one book alone in a few hours could make us all honest, compelling storytellers for the rest of our lives, you already know it doesn't work that way. Unfortunately, like everything else we get good at, learning the elements that make us good is just the beginning. Then comes the practice that hones our skills.

If you're willing to be brave, then please do find some friends with whom you can practice your stories. Practice the good ones and the funny ones. Practice the stories you don't yet know are good or funny. No surprise, you will experience that whether your stories grow better or not, you'll grow closer, more connected with others. You'll build friendships. And in the end, that's far better than just crafting better stories.

Stories can be great. Friendships are way better. Whatever you do, please use what you have learned from me to grow strong relationships. That's what storytelling for leadership comes down to. If you do that, then our plan is working and I'm delighted we could come together.

My team helps me create work that strengthens others and share it with the world. We only know if our plan works when you tell us.

You can contact my team and find resources to help you go deeper at CharlesVogl.com

Go inspire laughs, hugs, and tears.
Godspeed.

— Charles Vogl
   Oakland, CA

Suggested Reading

Brené Brown, Daring Greatly: How the Courage to Be Vulnerable Transforms the Way We Live, Love, Parent, and Lead (New York: Avery, 2012).

Joseph Campbell, The Hero of a Thousand Faces, 3rd ed (Novato, CA: New World Library, 2008).

Marshall Ganz. What Is Public Narrative: Self, Us & Now (Public Narrative Worksheet). Working Paper. (2009).

Marshall Ganz. Why Stories Matter. Sojourners (March 2009).

Robert McKee, Story: Substance, Structure, Style and the Principles of Screenwriting (New York: HarperCollins, 1997).

Scott McCloud, Understanding Comics: The Invisible Art (New York: William Morrow, 1994).

APPRECIATION AND ACKNOWLEDGMENT TO THOSE WHO SUPPORTED SHARING THIS WITH THE WORLD

Patricia Alejandro
Mark Boyce
Dai & Betty Chang
Kari Chisholm
Bjorn Cooley
Kori Crockett
Amit Garg
Gabriel Grant
Jason Harp
Steven Hiatt
Tokunboh Ishmael
Kurt Johnson
Emily Levada
Socheata Poeuv
Uma Ramiah
John Mabry
Leandro Margulis

Rose-Anne Moore
Victor Mutai
Stephanie Noble
Alastair Ong
Alan Price
Beth Quitman
Uma Ramiah
Yulian Ramos
Casey Rosengren
Daniel Schier
James Vogl
Richard & Marcia Vogl
Marvin K. White
Annu Yadav
Laura Yates

The friends who trusted me with your stories and prefer anonymity.

The kind people at the coffee and bakery on 40th St. who let me sit for many hours.

And Friday & Hanu dogs who kept me company through so many months.

May we change the world one word at a time.

NOTES

1   CIGNA 2018 U.S. Loneliness Index
2   Marshall Ganz. Why Stories Matter. March, 2009
3   The Lord of the Rings: The Fellowship of the Ring., Written by Fran Walsh, Philippa Boyens and Peter Jackson, New Line Cinema, 2001
4   Jerome S. Bruner, *Making Stories: Law, Literature, Life* (Cambridge, MA: Harvard University Press, 2003).
5   J. A. Easterbrook, "The Effect of Emotion on Cue Utilization and the Organization of Behavior," *Psychological Review* 66:3 (1959): 183–201. doi:10.1037/h0047707. PMID 13658305; A. K. Anderson and E. A. Phelps. "Lesions of the Human Amygdala Impair Enhanced Perception of Emotionally Salient Events," *Nature* 411 (17 May 2001): 305–9. doi:10.1038/35077083. PMID 11357132.
6   Jonathan Haidt, "The Emotional Dog and Its Rational Tail: A Social Intuitionist Approach to Moral Judgment," Psychological Review, 108:4 (October 2001): 814–34. doi: 10.1037/0033-295X.108.4.814.
7   Paul Slovic, "'If I Look at the Mass I Will Never Act': Psychic Numbing and Genocide," *Judgment and Decision Making*, 2:2 (April 2007): 79–95.
8   Shawn Achor, Andrew Reece, Gabriella Rosen Kellerman, Alexi Robichaux. 9 Out of 10 People Are Willing to Earn Less Money to Do More-Meaningful Work. Harvard Business Review website. Nv. 6, 2018
9   Campbell Joseph. A Joseph Campbell Companion: Reflections on the Art of Living. Joseph Campbell Foundation. Aug.1, 2011

10   Bill Moyers Joseph Campbell and The Power of Myth. Episode. 1: 'The Hero's Adventure' June 21, 1988. Note "we're not going on our journey to save the world, but to save ourselves" is a Bill Moyers quote summarizing Campbell's idea within the interview.

11   Bill Moyers Joseph Campbell and The Power of Myth. Episode. 1: 'The Hero's Adventure' June 21, 1988

12   Bill Moyers Joseph Campbell and The Power of Myth. Episode. 1: 'The Hero's Adventure' June 21, 1988

13   Campbell, Joseph; Bill Moyers. *The Power of Myth*. Anchor: New York. 1991.

14   Campbell, Joseph. A Hero of a Thousand Faces. Pantheon Books. United States 1949

15   Brené Brown, *Daring Greatly: How the Courage to Be Vulnerable Transforms the Way We Live, Love, Parent, and Lead* (London: Penguin, 2012), 35: "The definition of vulnerability is uncertainty, risk, and emotional exposure."

16   *Campbell, Joseph. The Power of Myth. Chapter 2. (Anchor) 1991*

ABOUT THE AUTHOR— CHARLES H. VOGL, M.DIV.

Charles Vogl supports leaders in for-profit, non-profit and civic organizations to make meaningful change in alignment with their core values. He draws from the realm of spiritual traditions to understand how individuals build loyalty, strengthen identity, and live out shared values. These principles apply to both secular and spiritual leadership.

He teaches how to build critical connections for leadership that impact generations. He believes that every effective leader relies upon a community of stakeholders on which their success depends. When leaders communicate their story in a powerful way, they can generate inspiration, excitement, and commitment in others. The right kind of communication creates relationships that are effective and resilient.

Charles began his lifelong study of stories at a Hollywood studio and then as a documentary filmmaker in New York. His PBS projects touch on topics such as education, school reform and civil rights advocacy. His film, "New Year Baby," tells the story of Cambodian genocide survivors. The film won many awards including the Amnesty International "Movies That Matter" award.

After his own work in human rights advocacy, he went on to study leaders in social movements, business, and spiritual traditions at Yale University. He earned a Master of Divinity at Yale as a Jesse ball DuPont foundation scholar.

At the Yale Law School, he co-founded the Visual Law Project which teaches storytelling principles to support justice advocacy. He is a regular guest lecturer at Yale.

His book The Art of Community distills concepts from 3,000 years of spiritual traditions so leadership can use them to create a culture belonging in any organization field or movement. It won a Nautilus Silver Book Award for Business and Leadership writing.

He lives in beautiful Oakland, CA, with his wife. In one year, he survived a plane crash, a spitting cobra attack, and acute malaria while living in Sub-Saharan Africa. Those are stories for another time.

CharlesVogl.com

LEADERSHIP STORY
7 MAGICAL ELEMENTS

- **Setting:** A specific time and place.

- **Characters:** The people involved.

- **Inciting Incident:** Something happens that causes a thought and feeling inspiring a choice toward a new goal.

- **Challenge:** Things to overcome to achieve a goal.

- **The "At Stake":** The important outcome.

- **Lesson:** Anything (especially wisdom) you learned in the story.

- **Bigger Idea:** How the story affects people other than the hero.

Printed in Great Britain
by Amazon

69603052R00177